Merthyr Tydfil Tramroads and their Locomotives

GORDON RATTENBURY
M. J. T. LEWIS

with 48 illustrations and 6 maps

RAILWAY & CANAL HISTORICAL SOCIETY

Cover illustration

Michael Blackmore's painting depicts the Dowlais Iron Company's locomotive *Perseverance* climbing the steep gradient between Penydarren End and Dowlais in or soon after 1832. The rack rail may be seen between the running rails. The twin chimneys could be folded back to pass through Plymouth tunnel, but the winch for raising and lowering them is not shown because its design is unknown. The locomotive wheels should have six sets of spokes, not the eight shown. The train consists of a tram carrying imported iron ore for the furnaces, a simple bogie waggon returning empty to the works for loading with long bar iron, and one empty four-wheeled tram for shorter bars. In the foreground is the Morlais Brook, beyond the train is the Abernant–Rhyd y Blew turnpike road, and behind that rises Morlais Hill, now largely covered in housing estates. The painting was commissioned for the dual purpose of serving as the cover of this book and of publicising the proposal to build a reconstruction of *Perseverance* (as mentioned in the introduction to Michael Lewis's contribution).

First published 2004 by the Railway & Canal Historical Society

The Railway & Canal Historical Society was founded in 1954 and incorporated in 1967. It is a company (No.922300) limited by guarantee and registered in England as a charity (No.256047) Registered office: 3 West Court, West Street, Oxford OX2 0NP

Gordon Rattenbury's text © 2004 John Rattenbury

M. J. T. Lewis's text © 2004 M. J. T. Lewis

All rights reserved
No part of this publication may be reproduced or transmitted
in any form or by any means without the prior written permission of the publisher

ISBN 0 901461 52 0

Designed and typeset by Malcolm Preskett
Printed in England by Biddles Ltd, King's Lynn

Contents

Foreword 4
Editor's introduction 5

The History — by Gordon Rattenbury
The Ironworks and the Canal 9
Dowlais Railroad 11
Penydarren Ironworks Tramroads 16
Dowlais Iron Company's Limestone Tramroads 23
Gurnos Tramroad 26
Merthyr Tramroad Company (The Penydarren Tramroad) 30

The Locomotives — by M. J. T. Lewis
Introduction 46
The Tramroads 47
Penydarren Company Locomotives 51
Trevithick's locomotive • The Stephenson locomotive
Cyfarthfa Ironworks Locomotives 58
Hirwaun • The Williams locomotive • The Gurney locomotives
The Neath Abbey locomotive
Dowlais Iron Company Locomotives 63
Neath Abbey • *Perseverance* • *Yn Barod Etto* • *Mountaineer* • *Dowlais*
Charles Jordan • *John Watt* • General remarks
A Trip behind 'Perseverance' 80
APPENDIX: Summary List of Locomotives 85

Notes and References 86
Index 88

Foreword

It is very fitting that the Railway & Canal Historical Society should be publishing two books in 2004 to commemorate the 200th anniversary of the first steam locomotive to pull a loaded train along rails anywhere in the world and also the 50th anniversary of the founding of the Society in 1954.

Appropriately the first book is about the Merthyr Tramroad and its locomotives. The first of these was Trevithick's steam locomotive which made history on 13 February 1804, thus heralding the start of the Railway Age which brought about the biggest programme of heavy construction then known in the United Kingdom.

The only earlier but much smaller parallel had been the construction of the canals and it is right that our second volume, entitled *Canal Boatmen's Missions* deals with a fascinating but hitherto little known area of activity among the men and women who worked on the 'cut'.

I commend both of these volumes to you and hope that if you are not already a member of our Society you will quickly become one. We also welcome suitable manuscripts for consideration by the Publications Committee for possible publication under the aegis of the Society.

Ian Markey
Chairman
Railway & Canal Historical Society
Publications Committee

Editor's introduction

Merthyr Tydfil was one of the phenomena of the Industrial Revolution. A small and isolated village in the middle of the eighteenth century, by 1801, within little more than thirty years, it had become the largest urban settlement in Wales. This explosive expansion was all due to the growth of the iron industry for which Merthyr, on the very northern outcrop of the south Wales coalfield, was an ideal location. Rich reserves of coal and iron ore were to be found on one side and an equal abundance of easily quarried limestone just a mile or so to the north. The town itself lies in the valley of the river Taff, just below the confluence of its two main tributaries, the Taf Fawr and the Taf Fechan. Both rise in the Brecon Beacons whose prodigal rainfall ensured that except in the driest of summers they could always be counted on as an unfailing source of water power.

By the end of the eighteenth century four ironworks had located themselves in and around Merthyr – Cyfarthfa, Penydarren, Plymouth and, a little further out, Dowlais. The demands of an industrialising economy and the frequent occurrence of war ensured that they flourished and expanded. There was only one thing that detracted from their success: the nearest navigable water was 25 miles away at Cardiff, and in the eighteenth century access to navigable water was essential for the successful distribution of any product. Land transport was slow and inefficient. If the ironworks were to realise their full potential, it was essential that a reliable and cost-effective route should be established between the ironworks of Merthyr and the sea at Cardiff.

The ironmasters' first attempt at improving their communications was a turnpike road of limited capacity. The Glamorganshire Canal of 1794 was a great improvement on this, but a severe drop in height was required, especially in the upper sections, and the numerous locks that were needed to achieve this were a constant source of delay to the traffic. Consequently the owners of three of the ironworks, Dowlais, Penydarren and Plymouth, combined to built a tramroad from the ironworks to the modern Abercynon which would by-pass the most difficult section of the canal. This tramroad, the Merthyr Tramroad, sometimes less correctly known as the Penydarren Tramroad, was opened in 1802.

The Merthyr Tramroad and its locomotives are the subject of the present book. In the first part the late Gordon Rattenbury describes the steps which led to its formation and recounts its continuing history until its final demise. He also deals with the history of the associated railroads and tramroads in and around Merthyr which served to link the various ironworks to the Glamorganshire Canal and to the quarries from which they obtained their supplies of limestone.

Whilst the Merthyr Tramroad was an important road in its own right, perhaps it is most remembered today as the line on which the world's first railway engine operated in 1804. For all that, Richard Trevithick's locomotive only worked for a few months and it was not until 1829 that steam traction reappeared. The events surrounding the construction and operation of Trevithick's locomotive and the subsequent locomotives are described in the second part of this book by Michael Lewis. His *Steam on the Penydarren* was first published by the Industrial Railway Society in 1975 and has long been out of print. His present contribution forms an extensively revised version of that work, including a totally new section on the early tramroad locomotives built or operated by Cyfarthfa.

In his account of the Merthyr Tramroad, Gordon Rattenbury deliberately chose to omit any but the most cursory mention of the locomotives because of the existence of Lewis's work. Conversely, in writing the historical background which formed the first part of his original work, Lewis was happy to acknowledge his debt to Rattenbury. The publication between a single set of covers of these two works is thus a very happy combination and a fitting means of acknowledging the importance of the Merthyr Tramroad on the occasion of the 200th anniversary of Trevithick's locomotive.

Gordon Rattenbury completed his manuscript in 1987 and it remained unpublished at the time of his death in 1990. Since then several further works have appeared which have a bearing on the subject. Had he been spared, the author would no doubt have given them his full consideration and modified his own work as he thought appropriate. The editor of the present work has made no attempt to carry this task out posthumously on his behalf, and the integrity of the text, as it was left by its author, has been respected. However, in order to ensure that the reader is aware of later work which may add to Rattenbury's work or suggest that in some cases a measure of re-assessment may be required, I have added footnotes where necessary to draw attention to later work. Footnotes also explain what might at first sight appear to be discrepancies between the two contributors to this volume, particularly in the differing conventions they have adopted in specifying track gauges.

The work of two later writers in particular needs be taken into account. These are:

Stephen Rowson and Ian L. Wright,
The Glamorganshire and Aberdare Canals, Volume 1, Merthyr Tydfil & Aberdare to Pontypridd,
Black Dwarf Publications, 2001.

John van Laun, *Early Limestone Railways: how Railways Developed to Feed the Furnaces of the Industrial Revolution in South East Wales,*
Newcomen Society, 2001.

In preparing this work for publication, my first debt, on behalf of the Railway & Canal Historical Society, is to John Rattenbury who kindly made his late father's manuscript available and agreed to its publication, and to the Industrial Railway Society and Michael Lewis, the former for agreeing to the re-publication of a work which originally appeared as No.59 of their *Industrial Railway Record* and the latter to devoting much time and effort to revising and enhancing his original work.

For permission to reproduce photographs and other illustrations I am grateful to Trevor Lodge, Neil Parkhouse, the Ironbridge Gorge Museum Trust, the National Galleries & Museums of Wales, Ian Allan Publishing, and the Science Museum/Science & Society Picture Library. Their contributions are acknowledged individually in the text. Hugh Compton supplied copies of photographs from the Baxter Tramroad collection in the Society's possession: it is believed that these were taken by W. E. Howarth for Stanley Mercer, the author of an earlier work on the Merthyr Tramroad. It has not proved possible to establish the present ownership of the copyright in these photographs and apologies are offered for their reproduction without permission having been granted. I must also thank my son Jonathan Reynolds for supplying a number of photographs of the tramroads as they are today.

The painting of *Perseverance* used on the cover is by Michael Blackmore. It was commissioned by Michael Lewis for other purposes and he has generously agreed to its use in this way. It greatly enhances the appearance of the book.

The maps were drawn by Richard Dean and exhibit the cartographic elegance which one always associates with his work. They are based on originals supplied by Gordon Rattenbury and Michael Lewis. In some cases these plans are taken more or less directly from documents in the Glamorgan Record Office, who have kindly granted permission for their reproduction.

The drawings of the locomotives used on the Merthyr Tramroad are the work of Michael Lewis himself and in all cases but one appeared in the original version of his work. They are based on originals held in the Neath Abbey Ironworks collection in the West Glamorgan Record Office. We are grateful to the depositors and to the West Glamorgan Archivist for granting permission for their re-use in the present work.

Finally I would like to express my personal appreciation of the advice, suggestions and assistance that I have received in particular from Michael Lewis and from Stephen Rowson in preparing this work for publication, and for the support of the Publications Committee of the RCHS.

Paul Reynolds
Swansea
September 2003

Merthyr Tydfil Tramroads

The History

BY
GORDON RATTENBURY

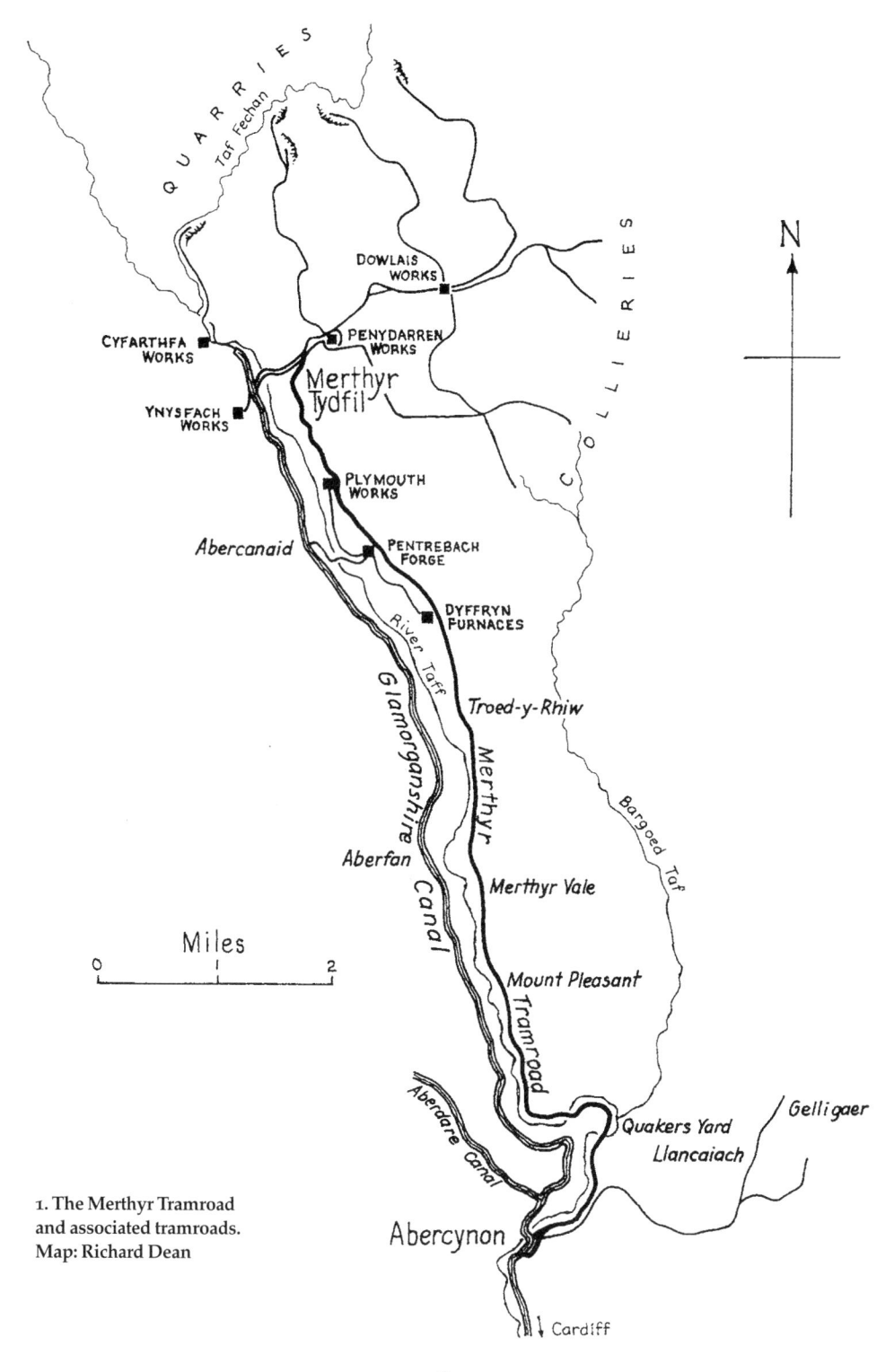

1. The Merthyr Tramroad and associated tramroads.
Map: Richard Dean

The Ironworks and the Canal

The first coke-fired furnace in south Wales was established at Hirwaun (SN 958057) in 1757 by John Maybery of Powick, near Worcester,[1] and in the same year the first steps were taken to found the Dowlais ironworks to the east of Merthyr Tydfil (SO 072077), when Thomas Lewis of Llanishen, Cardiff obtained a lease of land at 'Dowlass and Tor y Van' with liberty to erect furnaces. In September 1759 Lewis with eight partners, including Isaac Wilkinson of Bersham, signed 'Articles of Co-Partnership in Merthyr Furnace' to build furnaces and to trade as manufacturers of iron.[2]

In 1763 Wilkinson, in partnership with John Guest of Coalbrookdale, Shropshire established an ironworks to the south of Merthyr on land leased from the Earl of Plymouth (SO 055048). The lease carried with it a right to the waters of the Taf Fawr and the Taf Fechan rivers from Vaynor to Abercynon that had been acquired by Lord Plymouth under a lease from Lady Windsor[3] in 1765. The Plymouth works, as they were called in honour of the ground landlord, were taken over by Anthony Bacon in 1767, and Guest and Wilkinson moved on; Guest to become manager of the Dowlais works and Wilkinson to return to north Wales.[4]

Bacon, who originated in Whitehaven, Cumberland, arrived in south Wales in 1765 and by the following year had established the Cyfarthfa ironworks near the confluence of the Taf Fawr and the Taf Fechan to the north of Merthyr (SO 041067). Between 1777 and 1780 he took as his partner Richard Crawshay of Queenhithe, London, an established iron merchant.[5] In 1782 Bacon let the boring-mill, foundry and forges at Cyfarthfa to Francis Homfray of Wollaston Hall, Worcestershire who was joined in the venture by his three sons, Jeremiah, Thomas and Samuel. Within two years Homfray had quarrelled with Bacon and his lease was conveyed to David Tanner[6] of the Tintern Abbey wire-works, who later moved to the Blaendare furnaces, near Pontypool.[7]

Before leaving Merthyr, Francis Homfray helped two of his sons, Jeremiah and Samuel, to obtain a lease of land at Penydarren, near the centre of the town (SO 055068) where, with the help of capital supplied by Richard Forman, the brothers established the Penydarren ironworks. Their lease included mineral rights to the east of Merthyr, in some places making them sub-tenants to the Dowlais Iron Company.[8]

In 1784 Bacon installed his brother-in-law, Richard Hill, as manager at the Plymouth works, and when Bacon died in 1786, leaving his whole estate to his two sons, both of whom were minors, the Court of Chancery ruled that Plymouth should continue in production under Hill and Cyfarthfa under Crawshay in order to preserve the value of the properties for the beneficiaries. When his sons attained their majority they confirmed the leases to the existing holders.

The four ironworks at Merthyr – Dowlais, Cyfarthfa, Penydarren and Plymouth – had no difficulty in procuring their raw materials locally, but all faced a problem when it came to exporting their finished product. The nearest port through which they could export, either overseas or up the river Severn, lay 25 miles away at Cardiff. To reach the port there was only a pack-horse trail by way of Dowlais, Gelligaer, Senghenydd, Caerphilly and Watford on the line of the route used by the Romans to supply their outstations at Gelligaer, Penydarren and Brecon. In several places this climbed over the 1,300ft contour. Shortly after his arrival in the district Bacon was instrumental in effecting improvements in this route, but it remained slow and costly.

Under the Glamorganshire Turnpike Act of 1771 Bacon, Guest and William Lewis of Dowlais were among the trustees appointed to make a turnpike road from Merthyr to join the Cardiff District turnpike at Tongwynlais, about 4½ miles to the north of Cardiff; later, under the general Glamorgan Roads Act of 1785, Jeremiah and Samuel Homfray and James Harford of the Melingriffith tinplate works near Cardiff were included as trustees. Even by this route loads were limited to 2 tons and carriage was expensive.[9]

In general the ironmasters had their roots in the Midlands and they would have been fully aware of the benefits conferred by canals and their attendant tramroads, and it was natural that they should seek similar facilities for their new sphere of activity. Accordingly, by March 1790 a survey had been made for a canal from Merthyr to Cardiff, with a branch to pass Penydarren on its way to Dowlais. In June 1790 an Act (30 Geo 3 c.82) was obtained authorising the main line of the canal but omitting the branch to Dowlais. The capital authorised was £60,000 and borrowing was permitted up to £30,000; branches might be made either by canal or railroad up to a distance of four miles without further application to Parliament, and dividends were limited to 8 per cent.

The largest subscriber was Richard Crawshay with £9,600, and his family and associates provided another £8,500, together more than a quarter of the capital authorised, amply illustrating the benefit it was thought would accrue to the Cyfarthfa works from the venture. The canal was planned actually to wash the walls of the Melingriffith tinplate works at Whitchurch, Cardiff in which the Bristol banking firm of Harford, Davies & Co. was interested, and a further £5,000 was forthcoming from this source. The other ironmasters were not so interested: John Guest's son and his son-in-law, William Taitt subscribed £1,500 between them, thereby expressing their disgust at the dropping of the Dowlais branch from the Bill; and the Homfray brothers, with their backer, Forman, only provided £2,500, whilst Richard Hill, whose works, due to their location to the east of the Taff Valley, stood to gain least benefit of any of the ironworks, only subscribed £1,500. The remaining money came from bankers and landowners in Breconshire and Glamorgan.[10]

With its preponderance in the shareholding in the canal it was perhaps natural that the Crawshay party should adopt a proprietorial attitude, which showed itself in June 1791 when the committee authorised an extension of the canal by half a mile which would actually enter the Cyfarthfa works. Unfortunately the agreement for the additional construction with the contractor was not stamped, and in 1795 the canal company had to pay a fine of £10 to the Customs and Excise for their omission.[11]

The Glamorganshire Canal was opened throughout in February 1794 amid rumblings of discontent from the other ironmasters at the Crawshay domination of its affairs.

Dowlais Railroad

The omission of the branch to Dowlais from the Glamorganshire Canal Act of 1790 was a disappointment to the partners in the Dowlais works. For whilst it would have been difficult to work and to keep supplied with water it would, at least, have put their works into direct communication with the canal to Cardiff.

On 9 October 1790, only four months after the contract to cut the canal had been signed with Thomas Dadford and his fellow contractors, the canal committee received a request from Taitt & Co. of Dowlais and Homfray & Co. of Penydarren for a railroad to be made under the Canal Act to both their works from the canal. The committee thought it was a good

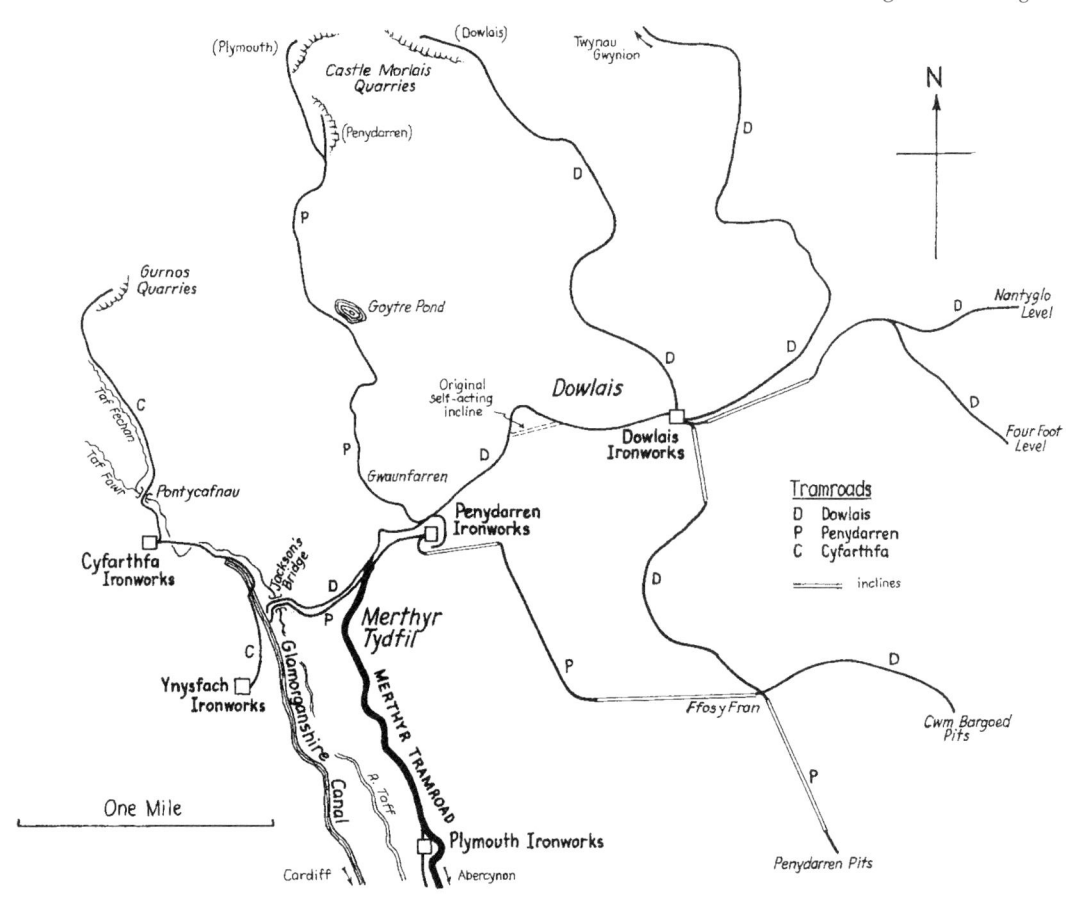

2. Tramroads around Merthyr Tydfil, *c*.1822.
Map: Richard Dean

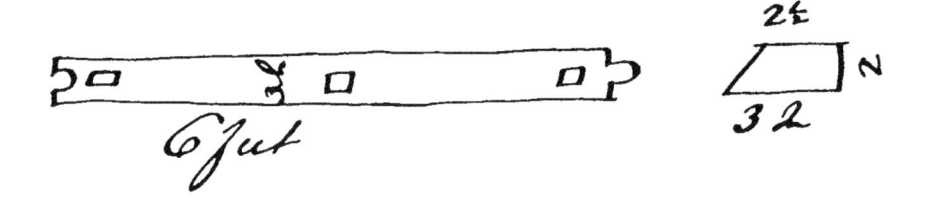

3. William Taitt's sketch of the rails which were cast in March 1791 for the Dowlais Railroad.

idea, but recommended that the ironmasters should make the line themselves, 'and when done to lay the Expence before a General Meeting of the Proprietors when the Committee will recommend liberal allowance to be made them by the Proprietors'.[12]

Legal authority for the acquisition of the land required was to be found in the 'four mile clause' of the Canal Act, and in May 1791, on being notified that the Dowlais Company was having difficulty in this direction, the canal company appointed five commissioners to deal with the matter in accordance with the provisions of the Act.[13] The canal general meeting in June 1792 was informed that the railroad had been completed from Dowlais to Penydarren End at a cost of £1,766 and it was resolved that the canal company would allow the Dowlais Company £1,000 towards their expenses, 'the same to be allowed them as soon as that sum shall become due to the proprietors of the said Navigation for the freightage of the goods of the said Dowlais Company'.[14]

It appears from correspondence between the Penydarren and the Dowlais companies in March 1791 that both Penydarren and the canal authorities had assumed that from Penydarren End to Dowlais the railroad would be made as a joint venture by the two iron companies, but the Dowlais Company had other ideas. In reply to a protest by Samuel Homfray that at Penydarren End the railroad had been built at too high a level to be used by his works, Taitt referred to the line as 'our Rail Road', and said that he could see no reason why Homfray should attempt to interfere with the line adopted; Penydarren might as well give their views on the manner in which the Dowlais furnaces were run. He pointed out that the canal company had not commented adversely on their plans

> . . . nor do they think that they have anything to do with it further than giving us what Sums they shall think fit towards the Expence of making it as far as your works. You forget that they do not intend to Contribute anything towards the Road from Penydarren downwards . . .

and that

> . . . Mr. Dadford (last time he was at Pwllywheiad) [i.e. Pwllyrhwyaid House near Dowlais, so 06310638] recommended the opposite side of the Brook to your Works as the most Eligible way to take the Road. This concurring with our Ideas determined us.

Taitt concluded his letter by stating that he trusted that Homfray would see 'the absurdity & Impropriety' of any interference in the matter.[15]

The only information that has been found in respect of the type of track used is contained in a letter from Taitt to a prospective customer, an iron founder in Newcastle upon Tyne, dated 17 March 1791, in which he stated:

> We are now making Rails for our new Waggon way which weigh 44li or 45li [44 to 45 pounds] per yard. The Rails are 6 feet long, 3 pin holes in them, mitred at the ends, 3 Inches broad at Bottom, 2½ Inches top & near 2 Inches thick.[16]

With a thickness of only 2 inches it is probable that the rails were laid on supporting timbers, in the manner of similar rails at Coalbrookdale, Shropshire.[17] That

---

* All the evidence is that such bar rails were self sufficient and not laid on longitudinal timbers: John van Laun, 'In search of the first all-iron rail', in M. J. T. Lewis (ed), *Early Railways 2: papers from the second International Early Railways Conference*, 2003, pp.93–101.

† van Laun (pp.45, 124, 134, 185, 204–5) shows that the accepted figure of 3ft 4in. is wrong and that it was really 3ft 8in. or possibly 3ft 7in.

‡ Rattenbury's measurements are back to back of the flanges: there is thus no discrepancy with the 4ft 4in. quoted by Lewis in the present work, since he measures over the flanges (see p.48).

the timber support would be necessary is borne out by the experience of the Monmouthshire Canal Co. whose 3in. deep rails were laid without support and who suffered a breakage of 702 rails on their Crumlin to Beaufort railroad between March 1793 and January 1794.[18] * No reference has been found to the gauge of the Dowlais track, but with Thomas Dadford, senior, as the engineer involved, it is probable that it was about 3ft 4in.,† as used by his two sons, Thomas and John, on the Monmouthshire Canal railroads and the Clydach Railroad of the Brecknock & Abergavenny Canal respectively.[19]

The date of completion of the railroad from Dowlais to the canal is not known, but it is not likely that it was before mid-1792 for two reasons. On 18 June 1791 the canal committee authorised the construction of a bridge over the river Taff at the company's expense, across which the two iron companies were to be permitted to lay their rails. Rails might also be laid alongside the road that the canal company was to make from the bridge (Jackson's Bridge, so 04570651) to the new road to Brecon (as it was then) at so 04880650.[20] Further, on 24 February 1792 Robert Thompson, at the time manager at Dowlais, writing to Taitt, stated that it was 'bad weather for the Rail Road, very little done this last week'.[21]

It is possible that it was complete by January 1793 when it was reported that the canal had 'for some time been navigated upon from Merthyr to Pwllywhyad'[22] (Pwllyrhwyaid at approximately so 088087, about 150 yards east of the Merthyr turnpike at Treforest, Pontypridd, and not the same as the previously mentioned place of this name). There is little doubt that it was in full use by June 1793 when the Dowlais Company was granted a wharf site to the east of the canal 'eleven yards below the Bridge at Lock No.1 at Merthyr' (so 04510647, the site of the present Drill Hall) at a rental of £2 2s per annum. The Penydarren Company was granted a plot for a wharf 'below the turning basin', adjoining the Dowlais Wharf on similar terms.[23]

Early in 1795 a Bill was introduced to improve and turnpike the road from Abernant (Glynneath) to Rhyd y Blew, near Beaufort, which passed through Merthyr. William Taitt and Samuel Homfray both gave evidence in favour of the scheme before the Parliamentary Committee. The canal proprietors were also strongly in favour and on 13 February passed a resolution donating their bridge over the Taff and the connecting road as far as the Brecon Road to the turnpike commissioners on condition that the iron companies' rights to lay their railroads were honoured, and that no toll-gate was erected between these two points. On 1 April the committee expressed the opinion that between Dowlais and Merthyr the new turnpike should be made parallel to the Dowlais Railroad, subject to suitable clauses in the Act to protect the Dowlais property.

The new road was planned to cross the Dowlais Railroad at so 05240686, near the end of the present Forman Place and the Trevithick Memorial. While the Bill was in Committee of the House Samuel Homfray managed to ensure the inclusion of a clause that gates should be erected on the side of the turnpike across the road to Castle Morlais and across the road leading into his works. The Penydarren Company was to be exempted from paying tolls at these gates, but the Dowlais Company was to be liable for toll if they travelled more than 100 yards on the turnpike.[24] The Dowlais Company naturally disliked these conditions as, should their railroad be out of action, they would be unable to reach the canal, the road to Cardiff or the road to Brecon without having to pay tolls.

The Merthyr (or Penydarren) Tramroad was opened in 1802 and to enable Dowlais traffic to be passed to it the Dowlais line must have been altered to a plateway to a gauge of 4ft 2in. (measured from back to back of the plates).‡ It is probable that once the line to Abercynon was opened, the section from Penydarren End to the canal fell into disuse; this was certainly the case by 1815, when, due to the collapse of one of the Merthyr Tramroad bridges at Quaker's Yard, the Dowlais Company was forced to transfer its cargoes onto the Penydarren Company's 'narrow Road' from Penydarren End to the canal.[25] The land on which the railroad had been made remained in the possession of the Dowlais Company at least until 1827, when

> . . . pieces of land which some time ago formed part of the original Rail Road made by the Dowlais Company from the Dowlais Works to the Glamorganshire Canal but which for some years past has [sic] been disused as such . . .[26]

were conveyed to the Penydarren Company.

From an opinion held in the Glamorgan Record Office[27] it appears that the land reverted to the Dowlais Company – probably on the closure of the Penydarren ironworks in 1859 – and was ultimately leased by the Merthyr Tydfil UDC in May 1893 to enable them to widen the road. Under the terms of

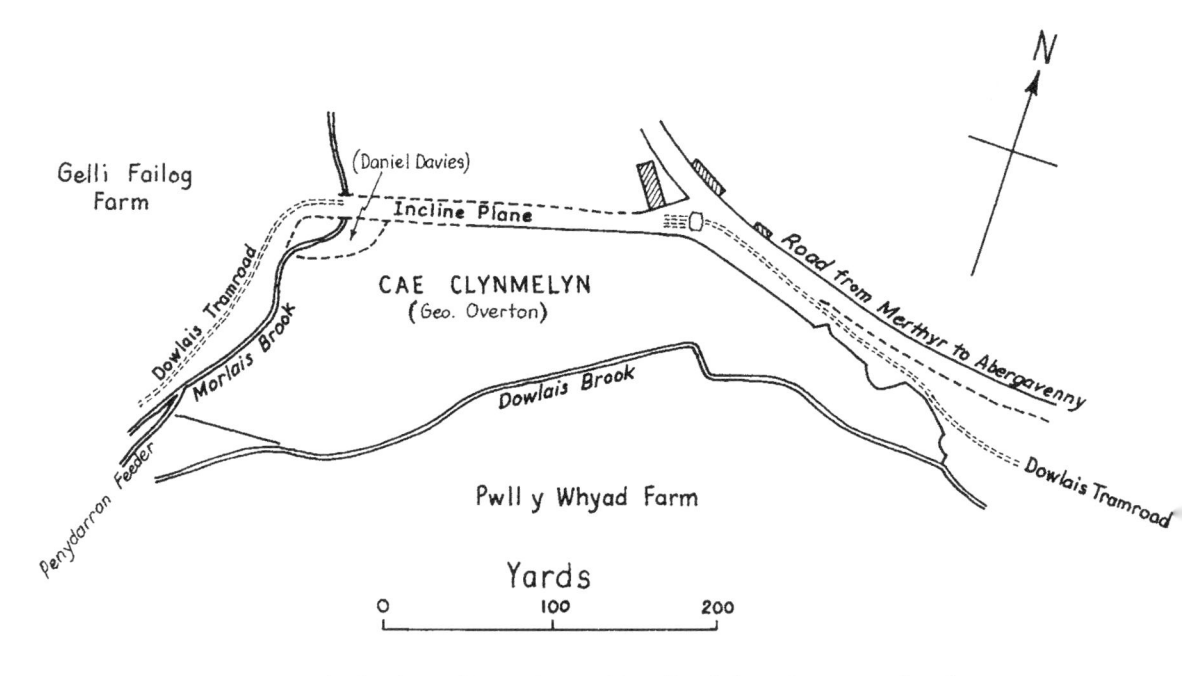

4. The original self-acting incline on the Dowlais Railroad shown in use on a plan of 1806.
Map: Richard Dean (redrawn from 'A Map of part of Gwernllwyn Isha Farm in the Parish of Merthyr Tydfil'
by John Williams, 1806. Glamorgan Record Office DG/P/222)

the lease the council was obliged to re-instate the railroad should the Dowlais Company require them to do so.

From its inception the railroad and the later tramroad were horse-drawn except for a self-acting incline about 200 yards long rising from SO 06050750 to SO 06240759.[28] A plan of Dowlais dated 1830 shows the tramroad to have been re-aligned by that date, and the incline is shown as 'old self-acting incline'.

It appears that by about 1820 the incline was proving to be too slow for the liking of an expanding works, and a slightly longer but more easily graded line was made over which horses could work the whole distance.[29] In 1832 advantage was taken of the easier gradient and the company acquired an 0-6-0 steam locomotive which could be worked either by adhesion or by a rack rail set 14 inches from one of the running rails over the more steeply graded parts of the line. In 1836 a second rack or adhesion locomotive was purchased from the Neath Abbey ironworks, but this appears to have been their last venture into this mode of haulage, and later locomotives were not fitted with rack gear. Both rack locomotives were scrapped or sold before 1848.[30] *

The tramroad from Penydarren End to Dowlais remained in use until the completion of the standard gauge Dowlais Railway brought the works into direct connection with the Taff Vale Railway in 1851.

As originally built, the Dowlais Railroad left the canal side at Lock No.1 and, after crossing Jackson's Bridge (SO 04570651), entered Bethesda Street on the line of the road constructed by the canal company and given to the turnpike trust. Keeping to the north side of the street it crossed the road to Brecon (later, but no longer, the A470) at SO 04870649 and ran on the line of the elevated pavement past the end of Merthyr High Street to Forman Place (SO 05230684) where the levels of the road and the pavement coincide. The height of this elevated portion above the roadway illustrates the difficulty that Samuel Homfray faced to connect a line from his Penydarren works with the Dowlais Railroad (FIG.5). It is probable that the part of the Dowlais Railroad from the canal to Penydarren

---

* But see Lewis, p.79 in the present work: they probably survived until later.

5. Penydarren Road, Merthyr, looking north-east from SO 052068. The original Dowlais Railroad ran on the line of the elevated pavement. When it was altered to join the Merthyr Tramroad it ran on the line of the former turnpike road. Photo: Jonathan Reynolds (2003)

6. Course of the Dowlais Railroad and Tramroad between the houses in High Street, Penydarren and the Morlais brook (SO 05600704), facing north-east. This area has subsequently been completely cleared. Photo: Gordon Rattenbury (1965)

End was abandoned once the building of the Merthyr Tramroad to Abercynon allowed the Dowlais Company to avoid the use of the upper part of the canal. Certainly this was so by 1815, as already related.

The Dowlais line turned sharply eastward at SO 05240690 to run parallel with the former turnpike road, the modern A4102, and pass over the Penydarren Company's tramroad to their Castle Morlais quarries at SO 05570702. Continuing to climb between the Morlais brook and the backs of the buildings in Penydarren High Street (FIG.6) it crossed the present day New Road at SO 06050743 to reach the foot of the incline at SO 06050750. When the use of the incline was discontinued the tramroad was extended to run parallel with Gellifaelog Old Road turning eastward at SO 06090768 to cross the Morlais Brook by what is shown on a plan of 1833 as 'Cinder Bridge'.[31] Turning south-eastward it entered Garth Lane, where the plan shows there was a passing place, and then crossed the line of the incline at SO 06230757, finally turning eastward across Dowlais High Street to enter the works at SO 06550756.

No records seem to exist of the precise locations at which the rack rails were used, but the steepest parts of the line were from Penydarren End to the modern New Road and from Cinder Bridge to the head of the original incline, and these were probably the parts where the racks were laid. Nor has any record been found showing why the rack locomotives ceased to be used after 1848.

Penydarren Ironworks Tramroads

THE abandonment of the proposed branch of the canal to Dowlais, which would have also served the Penydarren ironworks, and the quarrel with the Dowlais Company in respect of the route adopted for their railroad, left the Homfray brothers with no option but to make their own communication with the canal. There is no mention in the canal minutes of their having been given separate sanction for a line from their works, and it must be assumed that it was made under the authority given to the two iron companies on 9 October 1790.

The earliest firm evidence that has been found to show that the Penydarren Company made their own line to the canal is contained in an agreement with the Earl of Plymouth dated 20 June 1801 giving him the right to use 'a tramroad lately made' from the works to 'the Merthyr Canal'.[32] * An earlier lease dated October 1799 granting land to Richard Crawshay quotes as one boundary 'the Tram Road leading from Penydarren to the Glamorganshire Canal Navigation' but does not state the ownership of the tramroad concerned.[33] The use of the term 'tramroad' tempts one to assume that this cannot be the Dowlais Railroad, until it is remembered that at the time the terms 'tramroad' and 'railroad' were used indiscriminately irrespective of the type of track used.

In the 1801 agreement there is evidence that the Homfrays had already made a tramroad to their limestone quarries at Castle Morlais Farm (SO 055093).† In a clause authorising the Merthyr Tramroad Company to take stone from this source, as had been done by the Homfrays from the start of their operations, a penalty of £20 is imposed in respect of a tramroad made to the quarry without the Earl's prior consent. A regular supply of limestone would have been essential from the time the works was founded, and this was probably the first tramroad made by them, but the date of construction is unknown, and is certainly unlikely to be found in any legal document.

On 22 June 1803 the partners in the Merthyr Tramroad Company (the ironmasters of Dowlais, Penydarren and Plymouth) agreed to lay an additional rail to make the Penydarren Company's line to their quarries of mixed gauge, thus enabling trams belonging to both Dowlais and Plymouth to use it; ‡ from this time the line to the quarries was to be regarded as part of the Merthyr Tramroad for maintenance purposes.[34]

The line to the quarries left the Penydarren charging bank at SO 056069 and crossed the Morlais Brook at SO 05610701 by a cast-iron girder bridge, one side member of which remains *in situ* although well hidden by brick walls built to protect a dangerous waterfall (FIG.7).§ Passing beneath the Dowlais Railroad it crossed the erstwhile turnpike road and entered the aptly named Tramroad Lane from SO 05500701 to SO 05080726.

From the end of Tramroad Lane the tramroad ran past the Gwaunfarren swimming baths and northward up the valley of a small stream (FIG.8), which it crossed at SO 05080765 by a stone bridge which still survives to carry what is now a tarmacked public footpath beside the post-war Gurnos housing estate which it enters at SO 05200784. All traces of the tramroad are lost in the housing estate but it is evident that some of the residential roads follow the tramroad line. The 6-inch Ordnance Survey map of 1875 shows that from SO 05050816 to SO 04850828 it ran along the top of the dam of the former Goitre Pond, which has now been filled in and forms the playing field for a school.

---

* A possible date for the construction of the tramroad is 1796 (van Laun, p.172).

† van Laun dates the construction of this tramroad to 1799–1800 (pp.173–4); he discusses the design of the tramplates and the drams used on the Morlais (west) tramroads and the detailed development of these quarries on pp.170-82.

‡ van Laun (pp.151, 172) shows that Dowlais had ceased to work Morlais (west) by 1800: thus only Plymouth benefited from this third rail.

§ No longer to be seen as a result of road-widening work.

7 *(right)*. Cast-iron bridge over the Morlais brook that carried the Penydarren Company's tramroad (SO 05600701). Photo from *The Locomotive*, 12 February 1904, reproduced by courtesy of Ian Allan Publishing

8 *(below)*. Line of the Morlais–Penydarren tramroad approaching Galon Uchaf, Merthyr (SO 05070764), facing north. Photo: Gordon Rattenbury (1961)

9 *(top)*. Line of the Morlais–Penydarren tramroad to the north of the Heads of the Valleys road, facing north (SO 047087). Photo: Jonathan Reynolds (2003)

10 *(above)*. Trackbed of the Morlais–Penydarren tramroad, showing rows of stone sleeper blocks which carried the dual-gauge track that was in existence from 1803. The road has subsequently been tarmacked and the sleeper blocks are no longer visible. Photo: T. J. Lodge collection

11 *(left)*. Line of the tramroad to the Plymouth quarries at Morlais (west), looking north at SO 048095. Note the turnout. Photo: Jonathan Reynolds (2003)

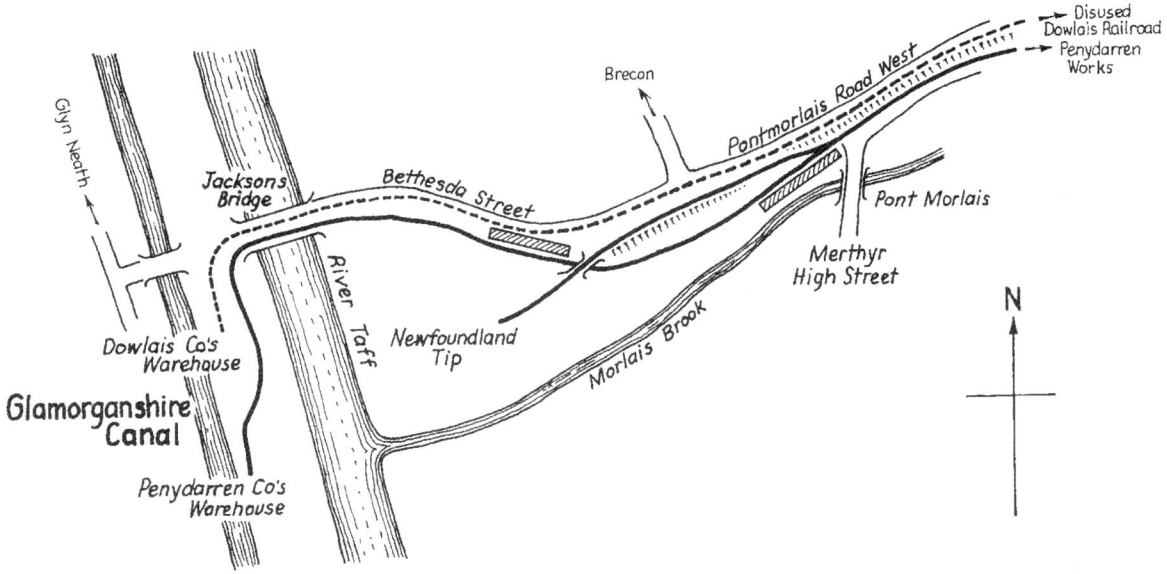

12. Sketch plan of Pont Morlais and Bethesda Street, Merthyr, 1833, showing the line of the tramroad from Penydarren to Newfoundland and Jackson's Bridge. Map: Richard Dean (adapted from Glamorgan Record Office Q/D/P/49 of 1833)

The tramroad can be regained by passing under the Heads of the Valleys Road at SO 04710869. Here it enters a narrow hedge-lined lane, in the roadway of which can be seen three lines of stone sleepers showing the mixture of the gauges that took place in 1803 (FIG. 10).* At the northern end of the lane it crossed the Dowlais to Pontsarn road to pass through a modern gate where it divides, the original (Penydarren) tramroad bearing to the east to enter their quarries at SO 048095, adjacent to the ruins of the 13th-century Castle Morlais; and the wider gauge carrying straight on to the Plymouth Company's quarries at SO 046098 (FIG. 11).

The Penydarren ironworks was built in the narrow valley of the Morlais brook, where the south side provided a suitable sheer hillside against which to build the furnaces. The site was long and narrow stretching the full length of what is now Trevethick [sic] Street from SO 056069 to SO 052068 and bounded on the north by the brook. Little now remains of the period when it was an ironworks, the site having in the course of the last 100 years been used as an electric power station, a tramway depot, a brickworks, and a bus depot since iron was last made there in 1859. Much of the site is now covered with houses.

The tramroad to the canal emerged from the works near the junction of the present Forman Place and Penydarren Road adjacent to the Trevithick memorial (SO 052068). It then ran on the south-eastern side of Penydarren Road and across the end of Merthyr High Street. On the northern side of Penydarren Road there is ample evidence of the reason for Samuel Homfray's discontent with the line used for the Dowlais Railroad in the elevated pavement that marks the line used for their railroad – about 4 feet above the roadway along which the Penydarren Company built their line (FIG. 5).

After crossing High Street the tramroad kept to the south side of Pontmorlais Road West and must have formed the access to the row of buildings on the south of the road at SO 050066. Dropping below the level of the present road it passed through a short tunnel under Abermorlais Terrace (SO 04890646) from which it emerged to run at the back of the houses on the south of Bethesda Street into which it ran at SO 04790648 (FIGS 13–15). It then followed Bethesda Street, across Jackson's Bridge, turning south at the canal side to enter the company's wharf at approximately SO 04550650.†

---

* This road has subsequently been tarmacked and the sleeper blocks are no longer visible.
† In recent years this area has been much modified as a result of road improvements.

13. Trackbed of the tramroad from Penydarren to the canal after passing under Abermorlais Terrace, facing east (SO 04830646).
Tunnel mouth in background.
Photo: Gordon Rattenbury (1971)

14. Trackbed of the tramroad from Penydarren to the canal viewed from over the mouth of the tunnel under Abermorlais Terrace, facing west (SO 04830646).
Photo: Paul Reynolds (1976)

15. Tramroad from Penydarren to the canal rejoining Bethesda Street after passing under Abermorlais Terrace, facing east (SO 04780645). The Dowlais Railroad ran on the left-hand side of the street.
Photo: Gordon Rattenbury (1971)

Where the tramroad fell below the level of Pontmorlais Road West, a branch continued on the level of the present road to SO 04880649 where it entered Abermorlais Terrace, climbing steeply to cross the line to the canal to get to the company's slag tip.[35] An idea of the size of this tip can be gained when it is realised that the whole of the district of Merthyr known as Newfoundland including a large school was built on it after the works closed.

Whilst it is known that the Penydarren Company's lines were built to a narrower gauge than that used by George Overton in the construction of the Merthyr Tramroad (4ft 2in. back to back of the plates) the precise dimension is unknown. In his *History of Railway Locomotives down to the End of the Year 1831* C. F. Dendy Marshall states that the gauge was 3ft but does not state the source of his information. Dr M. J. T. Lewis, in *Steam on the Penydarren*,[36] reproduces drawings of a locomotive intended for use on the Penydarren Company's tramroads, which show a measurement of 3ft 1$\frac{1}{2}$in. between the backs of the wheels, which would have been suitable for use on a plateway of 3ft over the guiding face of the plates, or 2ft 10in. back to back. Measurements taken in 1975 on the mixed-gauge section of the tramroad between SO 04700884 and SO 04910916 gave a distance of 2ft 9in. between the holes in the blocks used to support the narrow gauge rails, indicating a gauge of about 2ft 6in. between the backs of the plates.*

In February 1815, when the upper bridge over the river at Quaker's Yard of the Merthyr Tramroad collapsed, Josiah John Guest of the Dowlais works wrote to his uncle, William Taitt, stating:

> In the mean Time we shall send our Iron down, unloading it at Penydarran [sic] to their narrow Road & put a parting to turn into our Yard. I expect to load two Boats tomorrow.[37]

It is not known if this was a somewhat rare case of co-operation between rival ironmasters, or if the Penydarren Company's line, having been constructed

---

* See van Laun (p.174) and Lewis (pp.50, 55–7 of the present work) for further discussion of the Penydarren gauge. van Laun quotes a figure of 2ft 4$\frac{1}{2}$ in. over the flanges, taken from the diary of James Watt, junior, now in Birmingham Central Library Archives. Rowson (p.30) follows Rattenbury's 3ft.

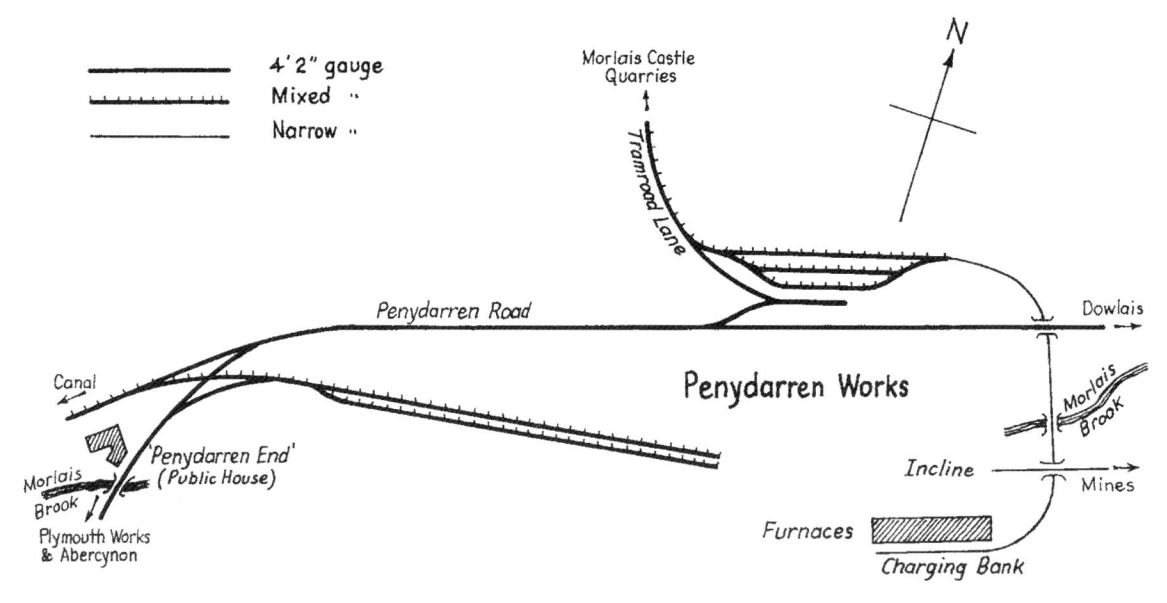

16. Diagram (not to scale) of tramroads at the Penydarren ironworks as shown on the Ordnance Survey 50-inch plans surveyed in 1851. Map: Richard Dean

under the 'four mile clause' of the Canal Act, was being treated as a 'public' tramroad.

It is evident from this letter that in 1815 there was no direct communication between the canal and the Dowlais works which would have enabled shipment to be made lower down the canal at Abercynon, a state of affairs that had probably existed once the Merthyr Tramroad had been opened in 1802. It also indicates that the Penydarren works did not rely solely on the Merthyr Tramroad for its export business. In 1827 the Penydarren Company leased the site of the former Dowlais Railroad from Penydarren End to the canal[38] and was enabled to re-align its tramroad by continuing the line to the tip from the bottom of Abermorlais Terrace to the original line at so 04790648 where it entered Bethesda Street. The tunnel was thus avoided, preparing the way for the locomotive they contemplated buying, which was too big to pass through the tunnel.

The purchase of the locomotive was necessitated by the need to import iron-ore, to be brought up the canal from Cardiff.* The Dowlais company was in a similar position in respect of its ore supplies, and it was probably about this time that a third rail was laid alongside the Penydarren rails to the canal to enable the Dowlais waggons to travel directly from the canal to their own line to the works at Penydarren End. The 50-inch Ordnance Survey plan of Merthyr of 1851, which was produced in connection with the 1848 Public Health Act, shows that the line to the slag tip remained on the narrow gauge.[39]

In 1849, as an inducement to the Penydarren Company to withdraw their objections to the proposed Dowlais Railway, the Dowlais Company leased them the site of the tramroad to the canal at a peppercorn rent for 99 years subject to it being kept as a tramroad. Penydarren was to maintain the tramroad for seven years, after which they might surrender the lease; in the event of the line ceasing to be used as a tramroad the land was to revert to the Dowlais Company.[40]

The Penydarren ironworks closed in mid-1859, but the tramroad from Penydarren End to the quarries continued to be used by the Plymouth ironworks until that works also ceased iron production in 1875. In 1888 the Dowlais Company surrendered the lease of Gwaunfarren Farm through which the limestone tramroad passed, marking the end of traffic from the Castle Morlais quarries.[41]

---

* It seems unlikely, for reasons of gauge and gradient, that the tramroad from Penydarren to the canal was ever locomotive-worked, and that this was why the tunnel was avoided: see Lewis (p.50 in the present work).

Dowlais Iron Company's Limestone Tramroads *

17. Dowlais ironworks in 1840.
Watercolour: George Childs, reproduced by permission of the National Museums & Galleries of Wales

UNDER the original 'articles of Co-Partnership in the Merthyr Furnace' each partner brought in property, either in cash or kind, for the joint use. The contribution of Thomas Lewis was his lease of land at 'Dowlass and Tor y Van' [42] which carried with it the right to erect a furnace and to take coal, ore and limestone. Geological maps held in the National Museum of Wales, Cardiff show that on the northern rim of the coalfield near Merthyr no limestone occurs south of a line from so 054093 to so 073093 – about a mile to the north of the site of the Dowlais works.

There are two plans in the Glamorgan Record Office, Cardiff each of which shows the part of the proposed turnpike road of 1795 from Abernant, Glynneath to Rhyd y Blew, Beaufort that lay between Merthyr and a point a little to the east of Dowlais. One is dated 1795 [43] and the other is undated. [44] They appear to be identical except that what appears to be a tramroad or a railroad has been drawn in on the undated copy; this leads from the works to Blaen Morlais Farm (so 07350935) which is shown on the geological maps to be the most southerly point at

---

* For a detailed discussion of the Dowlais quarries at Twynau Gwynion and the three tramroads that served them, see van Laun (pp.150–59). He dates the earliest to 1792: Overton's 1800 tramroad was the third.

which limestone is found. Whilst this was possibly intended to show the route adopted to get the stone to the works, the fact of the plan being undated limits its value as evidence that this was the original line to the quarries.

Writing in 1825 George Overton, at one time mining engineer to the Dowlais Iron Co., and engineer of the Merthyr Tramroad from Penydarren End to Abercynon in 1802, describes one of his activities in the Dowlais area in the following terms:

> About twenty-five years ago, I made a tramroad (of the same description with that which is used under ground, not more than two feet and a half wide,) from the Dowlais Company's limestone quarries to their blast furnaces in the parish of Merthyr; the total length being about three miles, and the fall about fifteen inches per chain [1 in 52½]. Upon this road each horse hauled regularly a weight of nine or ten tons, and took the empty carriages back. This continued to be the case for many years; in fact, until that road was diverted, and a new quarry opened.[45]

The descriptions that Overton gives in his book of other tramroads with which he was associated have been found to be sufficiently accurate to justify very careful consideration in this case.

At the gradient he quotes (1 in 52½), a line three miles long would rise by 302ft. The Dowlais furnaces were built between the 1,050ft and the 1,100ft contours, indicating that the quarries should be found at a height of from 1,350ft to 1,400ft. The Twynau Gwynion quarries at so 065103 lie on the 1,400ft contour and the distance from the works measured on the first edition 1-inch Ordnance Survey map and on modern 6-inch Ordnance Survey maps approximates very closely to the distance quoted by Overton – closely enough to justify the assumption that his line to the quarries was an extension of the line shown on the undated plan mentioned.

During his term as mining engineer at Dowlais Overton was responsible for constructing tramroads to the company's numerous collieries,[46] and there is little doubt that he adopted the somewhat narrow gauge of 2ft 6in. for use in the restricted space underground and then standardised it for general use on all the company's tramroads, above and below the surface.* This standard lasted for many years and as late as 1853 drawings were prepared showing waggon bodies suited to use on a 2ft 6in. plateway or a 2ft 9in. edge-railway.[47]

The 6-inch Ordnance Survey map of 1875 shows a tramroad from the Dowlais works to their Nantyglo Colliery at so 092082, a point now heavily opencast, which was opened in 1800.[48] From it a spur is shown leading to the level crossing at Dowlais Top station of the Brecon & Merthyr Railway on the line probably originally adopted by Overton to reach Blaen Morlais and Twynau Gwynion. Much of the line was later used by the Rhymney Iron Co. of Pontllottyn for their Rhymney Limestone Railway which has effectively obliterated traces of the earlier tramroad (FIG.18).

The quarry that replaced Twynau Gwynion is not so easy to identify.† In 1801 the Countess of Plymouth let the whole of Castle Morlais farm to the Merthyr Tramroad Co. for quarrying,[49] and it is known that both the Plymouth and the Penydarren ironworks obtained their limestone from this source after 1803. There is no evidence, however, that Dowlais was supping at the same table, and it is considered probable that by the mid-1820s they were seeking a substitute for their Twynau Gwynion quarries and had opened a new one to the east of Castle Morlais. J. A. Owen quotes the date of the opening of the quarry on this site as 1830,[50] but Overton cannot have known about this as he died in 1827.[51]

The opening of the new quarries necessitated the construction of a new tramroad. It left the Dowlais works at so 072079 and crossed Dowlais High Street, followed the line of Gwernllyn Road and came onto the line of the present Pant Road at so 06480827. It kept on that road to the quarry entrance at so 05990954. When the company opened the Ivor ironworks (so 056082) the tramroad was made to enter that works at so 06790805. The 50-inch Ordnance Survey plan of Merthyr of 1851 shows that the tramroad left the works by a tunnel at so 06510829 from which it emerged close to Barrack Row (so 06510839) whence it followed Pant Road to the quarry.

This was a far shorter line than that to Twynau Gwynion, being only 1 mile 78 chains from the furnaces

---

* van Laun (p.156) records surviving pairs of blocks on Overton's tramroad which are 3ft apart between the holes, which is consistent with 2ft 6in. between the flanges.
† van Laun (pp.158, 169) and Rowson (p.60) both confirm that the new quarry was at Morlais (east). The Dowlais Company started to work here in 1825, but road transport was used until 1833–4 when a tramroad, later to be converted into a railway, was built. Lewis (p.50 in the present work) argues that it was a railway from the beginning.

18. The Dowlais Iron Company's line to Twynau Gwynion quarries (on horizon) ran in the shallow cutting to the right. The later Rhymney Limestone Railway diverged to the left (SO 06750000).
Photo: Gordon Rattenbury (1976)

to the quarry entrance, and climbing only 62ft, an average gradient of 1 in 160.

By 1832 the Merthyr ironmasters, with the possible exception of Crawshay, were becoming dissatisfied with the service provided by the Glamorganshire Canal, and discussions were held that resulted in the Act for the Taff Vale Railway in 1836, (6 & 7 Will 4 c.lxxxii). The original plans show that Dowlais was to be served by a steep branch leaving the railway to the south of Merthyr.[52] The TVR was completed from Cardiff to Plymouth Street, Merthyr in 1841, and in the intervening period the Dowlais Company must have given a great deal of thought to converting its lines to standard gauge. It is not known what steps were taken,* but it was not until 1851 that the works was connected to the TVR by a line constructed by the Dowlais Company and known as the Dowlais Railway.

The 1851 plan of Merthyr[53] shows that the line was mixed gauge from the works to the quarry, the wider of which was probably to 4ft 8½in., preparatory to a connection being made to the general railway system. The 1853 drawings previously mentioned show that the narrow gauge continued to be used.

The opening of the Brecon & Merthyr Railway to Pant station in 1863 did not affect the Dowlais Company in any way, but in June 1869 the B&M was extended to a terminus at Lloyd Street, Dowlais – later known as Dowlais (Central) – and the Dowlais Company's tunnel was opened out to a deep cutting accommodating both the B&M and the Dowlais line from SO 06500845 to SO 06500832, where the iron company's line branched eastward to enter the Ivor Works, and the B&M continued to enter Lloyd Street.

In 1873 the London & North Western Railway's Merthyr, Tredegar & Abergavenny line was extended by way of Ivor Junction to the B&M terminus, and the Dowlais Company's lines were thus connected to the national railway system.[54]

---

* But see Lewis (p.78 in this work).

Gurnos Tramroad *

On 30 April 1792 the committee of the Glamorganshire Canal considered a proposal by Richard Crawshay that the company should construct

> ... a Rail Road from certain Limestone Rocks situate in the Parish of Merthyrtidvil at a place called Craig y guinas to join the Canal, conceiving such Road will be of considerable benefit and advantage to the Proprietors of the Canal.[55]

The committee approved the motion and ordered Thomas Dadford, senior, one of the original contractors for the construction of the canal to estimate the cost of the railroad and to submit his estimate to the general meeting in June.

In June the meeting empowered Crawshay to contract with 'any person or persons he shall think proper' to construct the railroad. In the following January he informed the committee that he had been unsuccessful in finding a contractor, and he was asked to do the job himself, presumably with staff from the Cyfarthfa works. He moved rapidly and the general meeting in June 1793 ordered that the minute of the previous June should be rescinded and that 'Mr. Crawshay having made such Rail Road at his own expence and agreeing to take to the same', ownership of the railroad should be passed to him.

The Plymouth ironworks, lying to the south of Merthyr, was in a poor position to obtain the limestone it needed to flux the smelting operation and had to rely on the Gurnos quarries (in Crawshay's possession) lying to the north of the town. While Bacon had been in control of both Cyfarthfa and Plymouth this had mattered very little, apart from the additional cost of transport to Plymouth. With Crawshay in charge at Cyfarthfa the family tie was broken, and Richard Hill had to rely on the good will of a rival ironmaster – and Crawshay would let nothing obstruct the prosperity of the Cyfarthfa works.

By the middle of 1793 Hill realised that he was absolutely at Crawshay's mercy. He wrote to John and William Powell of Brecon, his solicitors, asking their advice on how to deal with the situation caused by the building of the railroad. He informed them that it appeared that nothing could be done to stop Crawshay assuming ownership of the railroad as he was certain to hold sufficient proxies to sway the canal meeting in his favour – as indeed happened.

Hill's particular point was that he was in leasehold possession of a plot of land through which the railroad passed, and he wanted to know if he would be within his rights should he prevent the use of that particular part of the line until such time as he received satisfaction in monetary terms for its use. His letter concluded:

> [H]e has been found fault with on his charges (which are exhorbitant) and now he says I will take it to myself being a new offer of Power so congenial to his tyrannical disposition.[56]

When submitting the case for Counsel's opinion the solicitors pointed out that:

1. Crawshay had made the railroad without seeking the permission of the landowners through whose property it passed and had offered no recompense for its use. Mistakenly, the landowners had thought that the canal Act gave him the power to do so, and accordingly had not protested.

2. Originally Hill had been permitted to use the railroad, but recently he had been forbidden its use where it passed through Cyfarthfa land.

3. As made the railroad did not reach the canal, and any limestone carried on it only went as far as

---

* van Laun (pp.183–7) discusses this tramroad. From the evidence of the surviving stone blocks he identifies four different phases of construction, the original railroad and three subsequent tramroad phases. Lewis (p.61 in the present work) dates the second of these tramroads to 1830–31.

19. Gurnos Tramroad north of Cefn bridge looking south (SO 036079). The Taff Fechan is on its right.
Photo: Jonathan Reynolds (2003)

Cyfarthfa, and was of no advantage to the canal company. Crawshay had stated that he intended to continue it to the canal.

4. The original intention had been that Crawshay should construct the railroad on behalf of the canal company as a line open to the public. The canal company had recently declared Crawshay to be its sole owner.

5. Hill contended that the canal Act only authorised railroads to be made in order to carry goods to or from the canal. He had given notice to the Cyfarthfa hauliers to keep off his land.

Counsel's opinion was required on two points:

1. Did Hill have a good case to charge Crawshay's hauliers with trespass and could the same charge be brought against Crawshay himself?

2. If and when the railroad was continued to the canal, would Crawshay be justified in carrying over it goods not intended for onward carriage by canal?

Counsel, Thomas Caldecott of Hereford, gave his opinion on 25 July 1793 and suggested that Hill should erect strong fences where the railroad entered and left his land, and should demand that Crawshay remove the rails between these two points forthwith. He considered that if the railroad had been made in good faith under the canal Act there could be no objection to the carriage of goods not intended to be passed to the canal provided that this constituted only a small proportion of the total traffic. Should the railroad not be continued to the canal there would be an evasion of the terms of the Act.[57]

Counsel's opinion appears to have been passed on to Crawshay, who wrote to Hill on 5 August 1793 stating that he still considered that the railroad had been made under the canal Act and that his use of it complied with its terms; the land had been valued and he would pay for it 'to those who have a right to receive it – you I think have none – its with Lord Plymouth'. Hill forwarded a copy of the letter from 'the Tyrant' to the solicitor, pointing out that as his lease had seventy years to run Lord Plymouth was unlikely to be particularly interested. Hill copied a postscript that Crawshay had written on the back of his letter:

[I]f I may advise you for both our comforts let's end hostilities which can do no good. Every breach of civility only widens [illegible, possibly 'the gorge'] that will ere long come under sedate discussion You may be accommodated with stone or anything else in my power by civil treatment but nothing by compulsion.[58]

Probably as near to being conciliatory as Crawshay ever came with a rival in trade.

Following these exchanges a certain calm descended on proceedings, and in February 1795 Crawshay agreed to supply Hill for 65 years with 'good and proper ffurnace Lime Stone' delivered on the side of the canal at the warehouse in Merthyr for 1s 9d per ton.[59] At the time the normal royalty for quarrying limestone was 2d per ton, and even if it was costing Crawshay 6d per ton for extraction he was charging Hill 1s 1d for carriage over $1\frac{1}{4}$ miles of railroad, or $10\frac{1}{2}$d per ton per mile: under the canal Act, which Crawshay claimed was his authority to build the railroad, the maximum tonnage he was authorised to charge was 2d per ton per mile.[60] No wonder Hill considered his charges exorbitant, particularly as he had, in addition, to pay for carriage from Cyfarthfa to Plymouth!

Hill's worries came to the fore again in mid-1797 when he wrote to the solicitors in Brecon pointing out that under the canal Act 'all the Roads and Ways belonging to the said Company . . . (except the towing-paths)' were to be open for the use of the public free of toll provided that goods carried over them had been carried on the canal or were intended for such carriage.[61] On Richard Crawshay's personal copy of the Act there is a pencil note against this clause stating it to be 'an error'.[62]

As the road from the Brecon Road across Jackson's Bridge to the canal had been made by the canal company, Hill enjoyed free use of it to pick up his limestone from the canal warehouse at Merthyr under his agreement of 1795 with Crawshay. With that gentleman claiming ownership of the railroad, Hill was afraid that the privilege might be withdrawn as he was not collecting canal-carried goods.

In his letter to the solicitors Hill pointed out that he had, while the Bill for the Abernant–Rhydyblew Turnpike was under discussion, protested to Samuel Homfray that he would be in danger of losing this advantage. As a result the Act, as passed, had confirmed that goods passing over this part of the road to or from the canal were to be exempted from toll in spite of its having been taken over by the turnpike trustees. If, due to Crawshay's claim, he were to have to pay toll there he would incur a further £100 per annum transport costs.[63] From this letter it would appear that Hill's limestone was carried by road from Merthyr to Plymouth; it raises doubts whether the Abercanaid Basin and the tramroad thence to Plymouth yet existed.

Whilst Hill was assured of a supply of limestone by his agreement with Crawshay, he still considered he was paying too much for it. On 14 January 1799 he wrote to the Powells asking them to examine their records to ascertain if, as he thought, he had concluded an agreement with Bacon under which he was to receive stone from Gurnos delivered at his works for 1s 6d per ton. He asked them to treat the matter as urgent and to send their reply by the messenger who had taken his letter to Brecon.[64] Apparently the solicitors were unable to find any such agreement, and it may well have been the difficulties with his limestone supplies as well as his general dissatisfaction with the canal management that induced Hill and his elder son, also Richard, who had by this time joined him in the works, to sign an agreement with Taitt of Dowlais and Jeremiah Homfray of Penydarren on 18 January 1799 that the three iron companies should jointly construct a tramroad from 'the Lime Stone Rocks at Castle Morlais to Craig Evan Leyson' (the hill to the east of the canal basin at Abercynon, or Navigation as it was then known) which would pass close to his works.

The Merthyr (or Penydarren) Tramroad was opened in 1802, and on 22 June 1803 the three iron companies agreed to alter the tramroad from Penydarren End to the Morlais quarries to a mixed gauge by laying rails to the gauge of the Merthyr Tramroad (4ft 2in.) outside the Penydarren Company's narrower line. The expenses of the alteration were to be borne equally by the three companies but the value of the existing line should be regarded as part of the Penydarren contribution. Richard Hill was to be allowed £150 for actually performing the work, which was to be completed by Christmas Day 1803. Probably Hill obtained all his limestone from this source from early 1804.[65] The fate of his agreement with Crawshay of 1795 is unknown but it still had 55 years to run.

Under the lease from the Plymouth estate of the land on which the Merthyr end of the Merthyr Tramroad was constructed, dated 1801,[66] the Penydarren works was obliged to obtain all its limestone from Castle Morlais quarries, paying a royalty of 2d per long ton on all stone taken. It is probable that a similar agreement was made with Hill. With the tonnage on limestone carried on the Merthyr Tramroad agreed to be 1d per ton per mile, Hill was able to effect a considerable reduction in his costs, and in addition to have the benefit of transport right into his works.

The Gurnos Tramroad continued to be used for the limestone traffic to Cyfarthfa, and when Cyfarthfa Castle was built by Richard Crawshay's grandson William in 1825, a steeply climbing branch was made from SO 03840739 up to the courtyard of the castle to facilitate the passage of supplies. The 50-inch Ordnance Survey plan of Merthyr of 1851 [67] shows that by that date a coal yard had been established at the junction of the branch with the line to the quarry, and that there was a limestone wharf between this point and the river Taf Fechan. It is not known if these were enterprises of the Crawshay family or if other parties were by this time carrying on the railroad.*

---

* The track appears still to be have been *in situ*, if not in use, in the 1890s (Rowson, p.56).

20. Pontycafnau on the Gurnos Tramroad, facing north (SO 03760713). The siphon pipe in the foreground carried water from the pond in front of Cyfarthfa Castle to power water wheels in Cyfarthfa ironworks. Photo: Gordon Rattenbury (1974)

21 *(below)*. The replacement deck of Pontycafnau with cast-in tramplate chairs. The wrought-iron plates belong to either the second (1830–1) or the third tramroad.
Photo: Jonathan Reynolds (2003)

It will be remembered that at Richard Crawshay's instigation, the canal had been continued beyond its originally planned terminus right up to the Cyfarthfa works. The 6-inch Ordnance Survey map of 1875 shows the terminus to have been to the south of the river Taff and a few yards to the west of the present bridge in Cyfarthfa Road at SO 04150682. It is doubtful if the Gurnos Railroad was carried any further down the canal.

Recent developments, including the construction of an industrial estate on part of the site of the Cyfarthfa ironworks,* have obliterated the southern end of the Gurnos line and the nearest point to the canal terminus at which it can be located with any certainty is near Pontycafnau (FIG.20), or the bridge of troughs, at SO 03760713, so called from the trough built below the deck on which the railroad ran to carry water from the Taf Fechan to the works. This was the only notable engineering work on the line. Built to the designs of Watkin George, the chief engineer at Cyfarthfa, who had originally been a carpenter by trade, all joints are either dovetailed or by mortice and tenon – the type he knew best. Constructed some time between January and June 1793, it was probably the earliest iron bridge in Wales to be constructed for railed transport,† and unless another claimant appears, is the oldest one extant.[68]

All documentary evidence found refers to the Gurnos line as a 'railroad'. In view of the fact that Thomas Dadford, senior, made the original survey, and the early date of construction, possibly it was originally made as an edge-railroad in accordance with local practice at the time. However, the deck of Pontycafnau has plate rail chairs cast into it and there is still a length of wrought-iron plate *in situ* (FIG.21). Measurements taken on the bridge would indicate a 2ft 9½in. plateway measured between the backs of the plates. When and if a change was made from edge rail to plate rail will possibly never be known.

---

* As a result of a restoration programme carried out in 2000 the site of Cyfarthfa ironworks has been cleared and the very fine furnace bank has been consolidated. Pontycafnau remains the first point at which the railroad can be picked up.

† van Laun (pp.185–7) offers a reconstruction of the decking of Pontycafnau in its original form as a railroad bridge and estimates the gauge of the railroad as 3ft 7in.

Merthyr Tramroad Company (The Penydarren Tramroad)*

Richard Crawshay's attitude of treating the Glamorganshire Canal as being in existence for the sole benefit of the Cyfarthfa ironworks was bound to cause friction where the other ironmasters in the district were concerned.

In addition to his disagreements with Crawshay over the Gurnos Tramroad, Richard Hill, of the Plymouth works, had a long running battle with the canal company over the water drawn from the river Taff to fill the canal, water to which he had a prior right under an agreement of 1765 between the Earl of Plymouth and Lady Windsor.[69] On several occasions the dispute erupted into physical violence,[70] and was not settled until the canal company erected a steam engine at Pont y Rhun to lift water from the river after it had passed through Hill's works.

The Dowlais and the Penydarren works each had their own quarrel with the canal company. Over the years the iron industry had used the 'long ton' of 21cwt of 120lb (2,520lb) for its exports to ensure the correct quantity of iron (in statute tons) being delivered after any breakages in transit. They insisted that the long ton should form the basis for their charges on the canal.

The assessment of charges on the canal was a rather lax procedure relying on the weights declared by the ironmasters and open to abuse. It was, however, a method that obviated the necessity for the canal company to weigh goods, with a consequent saving of staff.

To the discomfiture of the ironmasters, on 4 June 1794 the canal company decreed that as from 1 July all tonnages were to be calculated on the statute ton. The ironmasters persisted in returning their tonnages on a long ton basis, and on 27 June 1798 the canal committee decided to enforce the 1794 order, and their clerk was instructed to take proceedings against the Dowlais works to recover any monies lost to the canal. The Penydarren Company was warned that unless they abided by the Court's decision in the Dowlais case they too would be prosecuted.

The ironmasters had their riposte ready, and on 20 December 1798 a special general meeting of the canal proprietors was held to consider an advertisement that had appeared in the *Gloucester Journal* on 24 September giving notice that it was intended to apply to Parliament in the current session

> ... for leave to make a Dram Road from or near Carno Mill in the County of Monmouth to or near the Town of Cardiff in the County of Glamorgan and for making a Branch from the same to or near a place called the Quaker's Yard to or near to the Lime Stone Rocks in the Parishes of Merthyrtidvile and Vaynor ...

The notice also covered a proposed branch to Abernant, near Glynneath, from 'the Aquaduct' [sic] at Navigation (now Abercynon). The meeting considered this to be an unwarranted intrusion into what they regarded as their province, and appointed Richard Crawshay, his son William, John Wilkinson, Godfrey Thornton and their clerk, Wood, to go to London to oppose the Bill in the House.

Opposition to the tramroad was organised to include the trustees of the Merthyr to Tongwynlais turnpike, and the support of the Monmouthshire Canal Company was assured by a resolution of their committee appointing one of their number to liaise with the Glamorganshire Canal.[71]

On 14 January 1799 'An Address from the Glamorganshire Canal Proprietors, (and the Commissioners of the Turnpike Roads from Merthyr Tydfil to Cardiff)' was forwarded to all landowners with property lying on the line of the proposed tramroad, pointing out that £103,000 had been spent to construct the canal, which had been designed to carry all

---

* For a discussion of the name of the tramroad, see Stephen Rowson, 'When did the Merthyr Tramroad become the Penydarren Tramroad?', *Journal of the Railway & Canal Historical Society*, 2003, Vol.34, Pt.5, pp.310–15.

22. The route of the Merthyr Tramroad now followed by a town-centre street known as Tramroadside North. The sign in front of the terrace of houses reads 'Tramroad Tce' (SO 050063). Photo: Jonathan Reynolds (2003)

the traffic of the various works; whilst dividends on the canal had so far only reached 5 per cent, once they had attained 8 per cent the Act proscribed any further increase and surplus revenue would then be devoted to reducing tonnages. After pouring scorn on any suggestion that carriage on a tramroad could be cheaper than on a canal, it declared:

> In short, it is designed to ruin the Canal Company; and the Deed Poll-holders of the Turnpike Road will never after have five per cent for their advance ... Whoever looks candidly on this attempt will see the injury done to two useful sets of men, viz., the Canal and Turnpike Road subscribers. A waste of lands to profit nobody! [72]

The tramroad Bill was read a first time on 15 March 1799, the promoters being shown as the proprietors of the three ironworks, Dowlais, Penydarren and Plymouth, with the addition of William Lewis of the Pentyrch ironworks, near Cardiff. The plans, deposited on 13 March 1799, show neither the surveyor nor the engineer,[73] but they do reveal that a comprehensive system was envisaged. The main line to Carno Mill (in what is now the town of Rhymney) would have been within easy reach of both the Dowlais works and the nascent Upper Furnace at Llechryd at the head of the Rhymney Valley. The branch from Quaker's Yard to the limestone quarries would have passed close to both the Penydarren and the Plymouth ironworks, with branches into both. The branch from Navigation to Aberdare would have served the Abernant ironworks, near Aberdare, from which a tramroad had already been planned to serve the ironworks at Hirwaun.[74] At Tongwynlais the main line was to pass within 250 yards of the Pentyrch ironworks. The canal company's fears were well founded.

At further special meetings held in March 1799 the canal company suggested that, as counter measures, the company should drop the limitation of dividend, should reduce all tonnages, and should accept the 'long ton' as the basis for the calculation of tonnages. Samuel Homfray for Penydarren and William Taitt for Dowlais approved of these measures, and at a committee meeting held on 27 March the canal treasurer, Patrick Copland, was instructed to remit the extra charges that had been imposed on Penydarren and Cyfarthfa in respect of the long and short ton dispute. Taitt and Homfray were not so happy when they learned that it was intended that all ironmasters were to be obliged to carry exclusively on the canal, and that rates were not to be reduced as much as they had expected.

To the relief of the canal company the tramroad Bill was withdrawn before the second reading, and the canal general meeting in June passed a vote of thanks to Richard Crawshay for his efforts in opposing it; Edmund Estcourt, who had represented the Monmouthshire Canal at the parliamentary proceedings, was to be presented with a pipe of wine for his help.[75]

However, their rejoicings were somewhat premature, as unknown to the canal authorities, on 18 January 1799 the three dissident ironmasters had signed a draft agreement to construct a tramroad 'from the Lime Stone Rocks at Castle Morlais to Craig Evan Leyson (provided the landowners consent)'. Noting the date of the agreement it is surprising that the parliamentary proceedings were allowed to go as far as they did, but they certainly provided a useful smokescreen to confuse the opposition.

Under the agreement the costs of constructing the tramroad were to be borne in the proportion of five-fourteenths each by Penydarren and Dowlais and four-fourteenths by Plymouth. The line from the quarries to Pentrebach Colliery was to be completed within one year of the start of construction, and the whole was to be finished within three years. When completed the partners were to

> ... carry all their Iron down the Road ... and to pay 1½ pence per ton per mile for the same ... all Coal, Lime Stone and Iron Stone at 1 penny per ton per mile – should either of the Parties so dispose of their Iron that it cannot be carried down the said Road such Party shall not receive any Interest from the Produce of the Rates of the Road (on Acc^t of such Iron so disposed of) but shall be entitled to receive his proportion of the Profit arising from the conveyance of any other commodity.[76]

Within ten years this passage of the agreement was to be the cause of considerable disagreement between the partners when Richard Hill opened a second works nearer to Abercynon.

It seems to have taken some time for the news of the agreement to reach the canal company, and it was not until 1 March 1800 (by which time construction of the tramroad must have been started) that the canal committee debated the issue and instructed the following letter to be sent to the three works concerned:

> Sir, – By order of the Canal Company I beg leave to inform you that they intend to oppose by all legal means the use of a Dram Road running parallel with the Canal for the carriage of Iron to Cardiff from the Iron works of Penderran, Dowlais & Plymouth, on which Works the Canal Company depend for carriage when they subscribed their property ... and ... they hope before this road, so injurious to them and the trade of the Country, is proceeded with it will be duly considered and a Meeting had before it be further proceeded on.[77]

A politely worded declaration of war.

The ironmasters ignored this letter and several following communications, and on 26 November 1800 the canal committee instructed Copland to give them notice that 'on any attempt to carry the road over our Feeder he has orders to demolish the same'. The feeder in question carried water from the Nant Mafon at Fiddler's Elbow (ST 094957). In order to maintain a level it was carried northward for about 600 yards parallel to the river which it crossed by an aqueduct at ST 09419628, before turning south to enter the canal half way up the Abercynon flight of locks. The tramroad was planned to run south from the aqueduct alongside the feeder and perforce had to cross it at some point, which was conceived by the canal company to be the Achilles' Heel of the tramroad scheme. The land over which the feeder was carried, on both sides of the Taff river belonged to Jenkin Jenkins of Goitre Coed who refused to sell out to the canal company. On the suggestion of their London solicitor the company approached Jenkins in a further attempt to induce him to dispose of the land to them, under the threat that they would call out the Commissioners to enforce a compulsory purchase should he refuse.*

On 3 March 1801 the orders to Copland were renewed when the canal company heard a disturbing rumour that there was a proposal on foot to include the tramroad in the Bill that the Monmouthshire Canal was promoting for powers to make the Sirhowy Tramroad, thereby diverting the iron traffic from Cardiff to Newport, which at the time was considered the important port. Thoroughly alarmed at this possible development the canal company instructed their solicitors to keep a close eye on the parliamentary proceedings.

William Taitt attended the canal committee meeting on 25 March 1801 and informed them that the contract to construct the tramroad had been let to George Overton and that, no matter what happened, it was intended to proceed with the scheme. He

---

* Rowson (p.165) shows that this feeder originated at Quaker's Yard, not from the Nant Mafon at Fiddler's Elbow. The 'aqueduct' is in fact all that remains of the original lower tramroad bridge which was replaced in or soon after 1815 following the collapse of the upper bridge (see pp.36–7 of the present work).

refused to give the names of the other partners in the Merthyr Tramroad Company, and the canal company ordered that the Commissioners should be called out. Whilst Taitt stated that Overton was to be the contractor for the tramroad, a letter held in the Glamorgan Record Office, dated September 1800, from a James Barnes to the Dowlais Company states that he was the contractor for the tramroad 'from Plymouth Furnace to the Navigation House'.[78] Taitt's reluctance to name the other partners appears to have been an attempt to cover up the fact that the partners were in negotiation with Jenkin Jenkins to purchase the land on which the feeder was located, and the longer that this could be concealed from the canal company the more likely it was to succeed.

On 28 June 1801 the partners signed an agreement with the guardian of the Earl of Plymouth (then a minor) for nine years to cover the period until he should attain his majority. Under this the partners were to make a tramroad from the quarries at Castle Morlais to the canal at Navigation (Abercynon). They were to be permitted to quarry limestone at 2d per ton, and indeed, the Penydarren Company was obliged to obtain all its limestone from this source. One clause in the agreement imposed a fine of £20 on the partners in respect of a tramroad already made from the Penydarren works to the quarries without the Earl's prior permission. Bound with this agreement in the National Library of Wales are thirteen leases covering about $3^{3}/_{4}$ miles of the land needed for the tramroad.[79] One lease covers a strip parallel with the river Taff from Craig Berthlwyd (ST 094962) to the Nant Mafon at ST 094957, which includes the point at which it was proposed to cross the canal company's feeder. Much of the remainder of the land that was required was already in the hands of the partners under their works' leases.*

At their meeting on 19 August 1801 the canal committee instructed their solicitor to take action against the tramroad partners, presumably for trespass, giving as their reason:

> As we understand Jenkins has sold his Interest in the Land to the Dram road adventurers it will be necessary to make them parties to a Suit in Equity. You will therefore please to obtain the names of the persons to whom Jenkins has conveyed.

It was as well to know whom it was intended to prosecute.

On 5 May 1803 Richard Hill of Plymouth and his elder son, also Richard, agreed with John Nathaniel Miers, of the Aberdulais tinplate works, and Amos Shettle to open a forge at Pentrebach, $^3/_4$ mile to the south of the Plymouth works. The Hills were to provide the site, valued at £500 per annum, and Miers and Shettle were to bring in capital of £20,000. Richard Hill, senior, undertook to secure to the new company 'the use of the Rail Way now made and which passes within one hundred yards of the proposed situation of the intended Works' at $1^{1}/_{2}$d per ton per mile for manufactured goods and 1d per ton for 'rough' goods, these rates to be guaranteed by the Hills even if they should cease to use the tramroad themselves. The new company undertook to take all the output of the Plymouth works surplus to immediate orders.[80]

With the onus on the Plymouth works to produce as much iron as possible it was essential that their limestone supply should both be increased and cheapened, which was impossible as long as Crawshay was their sole supplier.

On 22 June 1803 the three partners in the Merthyr Tramroad Company signed an agreement that a tramroad of the same gauge as that to Abercynon (4ft 2in.) should be made to the Castle Morlais quarries, 'the present Road to remain on the inside of the wide Road, and kept in repair'. Materials for the new line were to be provided by the partners in the same proportion as their capital holding in the company, the existing (Penydarren) narrow-gauge line to be considered as part of that company's contribution. The Hills were to be paid £150 for 'making and laying the whole Road', which was to be completed by the following 25 December.[81]

A new complexion was put on the relationship between the canal company and the tramroad partners when it was reported to the canal committee on 8 October 1803 that the partners had suggested an amalgamation of the two concerns on terms that would guarantee 8 per cent on the original canal subscriptions of £100,000 and 5 per cent on the additional £3,600 that had been raised. The committee's response was very cautious and they wanted to know:

a) the cost of the construction of the tramroad
b) whether all the land had been purchased or whether any part of it was leasehold
c) the cost of maintenance in the past year, the

---

* van Laun (p.173) gives details and dimensions of plates for the Merthyr Tramroad cast at Plymouth and Penydarren ironworks in 1800-01, which indicates when it was actually under construction.

receipts in the past year, and at what rate tonnages were levied

d) whether the canal company could depend on all the produce of the three works being sent out on the canal or the tramroad.

The committee met again on 17 November to examine the scheme further and Richard Crawshay was requested to confer with Taitt 'on the business'.

This questionnaire and the agreement between the Hills and Miers and Shettle provide the only evidence that has been found for a date on which the Merthyr Tramroad was opened, the agreement stating that on 5 May 1803 it was 'now made', and the questionnaire showing that it must have been in use for at least a year prior to October 1803, or it would have been impossible to furnish figures for the previous year's working. There is no further mention in the canal minutes of the suggested amalgamation.

The law suit brought by the canal company in respect of the crossing of the feeder lingered on, and on 28 February 1804 it was reported that Richard Crawshay had received a letter from Taitt suggesting putting an end to the litigation. In response the canal committee minuted that:

> It is considered that this letter does not convey our ideas. We have never invaded their rights. The penalty or rent proposed by us will go in aid of reducing the Tolls. Had the Dram Road not interfered with us the Tolls would this day have been 20 pr ct lower or 3d pr Ton pr Mile.

It is not known what damages the canal company was claiming, but they can only have been minimal as the tramroad bridge could not have affected the flow of feeder water. Some solution seems to have been found by 18 August when it appears from the canal minutes that the only outstanding matter was the apportionment of the costs of the action.

The story of the run by Trevithick's engine on 21 February 1804 has been told many times, romanticised by the supposed wager on its success between Homfray and one of the other ironmasters. Many of the accounts lead one to suppose that only one journey was made, but Dr M. J. T. Lewis has shown that it made at least four journeys to Abercynon.[82] The engine was by no means a failure but the cast-iron track was incapable of withstanding the weight of the engine and the hammer-blow inherent upon a single-cylinder machine. There appears to be no documentary evidence as to the fate of Trevithick's engine, but it was probably taken off its wheels and used for pumping at the Penydarren works.[83] *

It appears that the canal basin at Abercynon had reached its limited capacity by October 1809, when the Dowlais Company asked permission to let the water out of the canal between the basin and the next lock down for them to construct a coal shipment

23. Bridge over the Merthyr Tramroad at Pontygwaith (ST 08099775). One implausible local legend has it that the chimney of Trevithick's locomotive was knocked off as it passed under this bridge.
Photo: Jonathan Reynolds (2003)

* For fuller details, see Lewis, pp.51–5 in the present work.

24. The bridge over Guest's extension of the Merthyr Tramroad from Abercynon basin, laid on the towing path of the Glamorganshire Canal in 1809 (ST 08429479). Photo from *The Locomotive*, 12 February 1904, reproduced by courtesy of Ian Allan Publishing

25. The same bridge photographed shortly before its demolition in connection with road improvements at Abercynon. Photo: Gordon Rattenbury (1959)

basin of their own.[84] The canal company agreed and the tramroad was extended about 500 yards along the towing path to the new basin at ST 08319457 with their consent (FIGS 24–5). This was not accomplished without difficulty as is shown by the following postscript to a letter to Richard Crawshay from the canal clerk:

> P.S. The Dowlais Co. began to cut their intended Tram Road yesterday, through Mr. Homfray's Garden, who being informed of it, immediately came down and set a Gang of Men to fill up what the Dowlais People had been cutting & then threw all the Tools, Wheelbarrows &c. into the Canal.[85]

The extension was a matter of contention again in 1813. On 21 October the clerk was instructed to write to inform Taitt that 'the Canal Committee will not permit them to convey Iron along the Road which they applied for for the purpose of shipping their Coal'.

The clerk informed the committee on 29 November that he had complied with their orders, but that Taitt had replied that he intended to 'persist in his Intention'. The committee ordered that William Church, their solicitor in Brecon, should be asked to visit the locality to view the state of affairs there. Possibly with the idea of frightening Taitt, it was ordered that a copy of the minutes of the meeting should be forwarded to him. Taitt's further reply is not recorded in the minutes. It is not known if the extension was made by the Merthyr Tramroad Company as a joint venture or by the Dowlais Company on its own; it was in use for many years and is shown on the 25-inch Ordnance Survey plan of 1875.

The smooth working of the tramroad was interrupted on 15 February 1815 when the northernmost bridge over the Taff at Quaker's Yard (ST 09039654) collapsed while a train of the Penydarren Company's trams was passing over it. One of the horses was killed and the haulier and four persons who had been riding on one of the trams were badly hurt. Notifying Taitt of what had happened, Josiah John Guest, a grandson of the original John Guest, informed him that he had made arrangements with the Penydarren Company for Dowlais traffic to use their narrow-gauge line from Penydarren End to the canal with a turnout into the Dowlais Wharf to be inserted.[86] In a further letter to his uncle on 18 February he stated that it had been found some time back that the bridge timbers were in a bad state; an examination had also been made of the lower bridge at ST 09439629, which had revealed it to be in the same condition. He had

* Rowson (p.165) argues that both of the present bridges at Quaker's Yard were built in or soon after 1815, the upper on the site of the bridge that had collapsed in that year, the lower on a new alignment alongside the original.

consulted Mr Scale, the manager at Penydarren, and Mr Hill of the Plymouth works, and it was considered advisable to reconstruct both bridges in either oak timber or iron.[87]

It is not known if the existing bridges on these sites were built at this time.* Both are of stone with a span of 63 feet. The lower one is without parapets, and a photograph of 1906 shows the upper one similarly unadorned. Parapets have since been added to the latter.[88]

The Pentrebach Forge of Hill, Miers, Shettel & Hill started production in 1807 with Richard Hill, junior, as manager.[89] To facilitate working the Hills made a tramroad from Plymouth to Pentrebach with a steeply rising branch from the new works to the Merthyr Tramroad. They contended that as the produce of the forge did not travel the full distance from Plymouth to Abercynon it should not be liable to bear tonnage for that distance. The other tramroad partners could see that it would be easy for the Hills to put the entire produce of both works onto the Merthyr Tramroad at Pentrebach, depriving the partnership of tonnages over $3/4$ mile on all iron made at Plymouth.

It is probable that the quantity of traffic put onto the main tramroad at Pentrebach increased steadily and, on 5 October 1818, J. J. Guest wrote to the Powells of

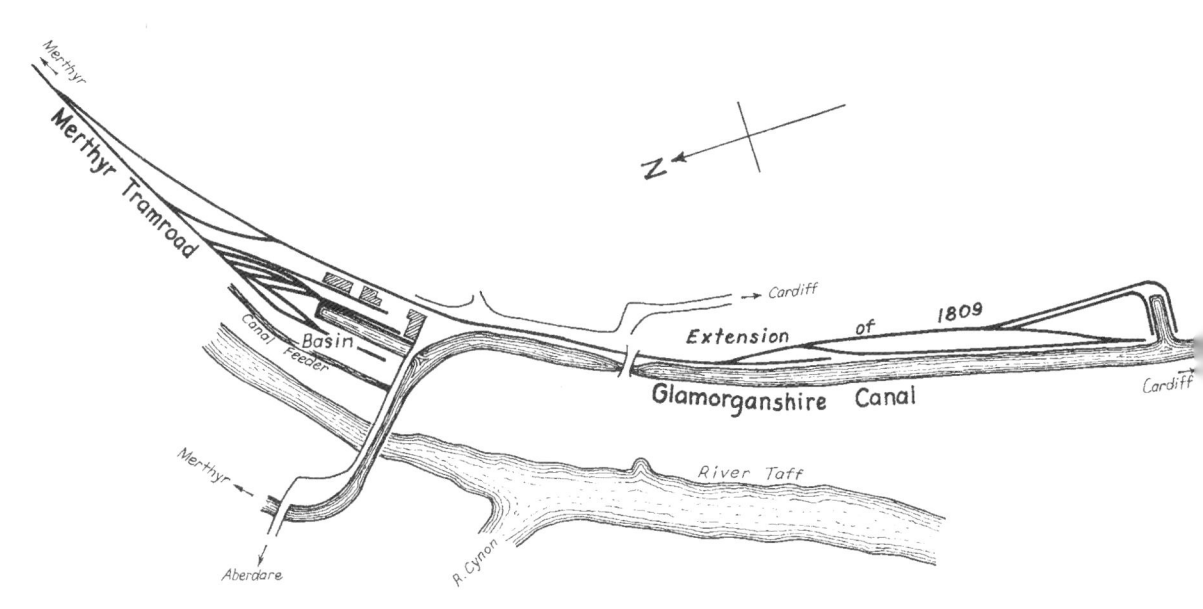

26. Sketch plan of tramroads at Abercynon, c.1870, showing the terminal basin and the extension of 1809. Map: Richard Dean.

27. Victoria Bridge (ST 09439629), the lower of the two bridges which carried the Merthyr Tramroad across the river Taff at Quaker's Yard. It was probably built in or soon after 1815 to replace an earlier bridge, which may have been carried on the piers beyond. Photo: T. J. Lodge collection

Brecon, the Dowlais Company's solicitors and those of the tramroad company, informing them that the Hills had refused to submit the question of their tonnages to arbitration unless Dowlais would agree to the same means being used to resolve a dispute of some fifteen years standing in respect of iron that had been supplied by Dowlais to Plymouth. The solicitors were asked to suggest a means of settling both matters equitably. In a postscript, Guest stated that the Penydarren Company would consider themselves liable to bear a proportion of the solicitor's costs.[90] In a further letter on 15 October, Guest reported that 'the Dram Road is now almost impassable', and asked the solicitors to write to Richard Hill, senior, who was responsible for maintenance of the tramroad, and to report the result to him.[91]

Hill & Co., as the Plymouth works company was known after the admission of the younger son, Anthony, to the business, replied to the Powells on 26 October thanking them for their offer to mediate in the tonnage dispute, but declining to settle it by that means. With respect to the repairs of the tramroad they stated:

> The present mode of proceeding – that of suffering the Tram Road to get out of repair and taking up one part to repair another – is a reflection on all parties. As men of business and from previous experience of such nuisance we would not suppose would have again been resorted to.

They also suggested that the time was ripe for the preparation of a new partnership deed for the tramroad company once the current dispute had been settled and the current quarter's accounts paid. On 24 December John Scale wrote on behalf of the Penydarren Company, giving their consent to the new deed being prepared and enclosing a copy of the former agreement between the parties.[92]

It was eventually agreed that Richard Blakemore of the Melingriffith tinplate works, near Cardiff, should be asked to arbitrate in the tonnage dispute having regard to the spirit of the agreement of January 1799 and the subsequent behaviour of the partners in their interpretation of it. His award dated 16 January 1819 was in the following terms:

> That it appears to me that however ambiguous the words of the agreement of 18th January 1799 are . . . yet I think the subsequent Conduct of the parties which I am specially directed to have regard to has put a practical construction upon it which in a great degree divests it of ambiguity or difficulty and enables me . . . to make up my mind upon the subject refer'd to me & I accordingly award as follows – that Messrs. Hill do pay the Tramroad Compy. Tonnage upon all the iron made at Plymouth Furnaces in the state or process of manufacture in which it is first away from those works . . . and that the distance for which such Tonnage be paid be for the Tram Road distance (as formerly acted upon) between

the Furnaces and the Forges – And that Tonnage be paid by Messrs. Hill to the Tram Road Compy. upon all iron made at and delivered from the Forges in the state or process of manufacture in which it is first away from thence ... and that the distance for which such Tonnage be paid be for the Tram Road distance (as formerly acted upon) from the Forges to the Basin.[93]

In other words, all iron sent out from Plymouth was to pay tonnages for the full distance to the basin, irrespective of its being routed via Pentrebach.

The only evidence of the terms of the original agreement between the partners that has been found is contained in a copy of the draft agreement extracted by Anthony Hill on an unspecified date. The terms of the second agreement suggested by Hill & Co. can only be gathered from subsequent events and correspondence.

It appears that the partners assumed management in turn for a period of a year. In a letter to Powell, the Brecon solicitor, on 2 February 1820 Anthony Hill stated that he had forwarded some papers to his brother, 'with whom the adjustment of the Tramroad business remains',[94] and on 11 February 1823 he informed him that he had forwarded the plans of a part of the tramroad to 'Mr. Guest who has been appointed Treasurer and Manager for this year'.[95] Throughout its life the maintenance of the track and the earthworks seems to have been the responsibility of the Hill family.

The preparation of the new partnership deed took a considerable time. In June 1821 Richard Hill wrote to Powell, asking him to forward the provisions that it was proposed to incorporate in it to Lord Plymouth's agent, a Mr Webb, as that gentleman was about to resign his position and was anxious to leave everything in order for his successor.[96]

Richard Hill was not entirely satisfied with the new partnership agreement as drafted by the Brecon solicitor, and in a letter to John Powell on 16 March 1822 he pointed out that a clause already agreed by the partners, that it should be possible to sue any partner defaulting in his tonnages in common law and so avoid 'the tedious delays of a Chancery Suit', had been omitted. He suggested that Powell should come to Merthyr to discuss matters.[97] This had already been suggested in the previous December in a letter returning a draft of the agreement written by W. Rowlands on behalf of J. J. Guest and signed 'for the Tram Road Compy'. Rowlands is the only official of the company, other than the partners whose name has been found.[98]

Hill & Co. opened another furnace at Dyffryn (SO 06930324) in 1820 and the private tramroad to Pentrebach was extended to serve it. At this point the Merthyr Tramroad was about 60ft above the level of the works floor, making it impossible to make a direct tramroad connection with it. Iron smelted at Dyffryn was taken back to Pentrebach to be put onto the main tramroad to Abercynon. Once again Hill & Co. contended that they should not have to pay the

28. Passing place on the Merthyr Tramroad north of Edwardsville (ST 08269711), facing north.
Photo: Gordon Rattenbury (1971)

29. Tramplates used at the start of a passing place, as in FIG.35.
The edges were scalloped to make the plates suitable for use at a level crossing, so that the wheels of road vehicles would not slip laterally when crossing the tramplates.
Photo: Gordon Rattenbury (c.1971)

full tonnages from Plymouth to Abercynon on iron made at Dyffryn, as it could not be said to emanate from Plymouth.

The managements at Dowlais and Penydarren had other ideas, and both wrote to the Brecon solicitors to enlist their help in finding an equitable solution. In a letter of 5 July 1822 Guest strongly advocated that Blakemore's award of January 1819 should apply and Hill & Co. should pay tonnages on their iron taken to Abercynon as though it had all originated at Plymouth.[99] Samuel Homfray, for Penydarren, forwarded a copy of the original partnership agreement and a very full statement of the origins of the present dispute, recounting that it was not until Hill & Co. had opened a second works and made a private tramroad to it that any claim for reduced tonnages had been made. He admitted that when the original partnership deed had been signed there had been no suggestion of any partner opening another works. It was his opinion also that Blakemore's award should apply.[100]

The outcome of any arbitration Powell may have used has not been seen, but in view of the continuance of the partnership it must be assumed that the Hills fell into line once more.

The partners in the tramroad still had to rely on the Glamorganshire Canal for their carriage from Abercynon to Cardiff. By 1820 the canal was so congested that delays to cargoes became serious. The congestion had been growing for some years. In 1814 the canal company had lengthened the sea lock at Cardiff,[101] and in June 1821 George Overton was instructed to examine the practicability of heightening the canal banks to increase the depth of water, thereby allowing boats to be laden more heavily.[102] On 5 June 1822 the canal committee decided to apply to Parliament for an increase of capital of £6,400 to be used to widen and deepen the canal and the sea lock.

The three ironmasters were very dissatisfied with the general state of affairs and both Plymouth and Dowlais refused to pay their tonnages for the last quarter of 1822.[103] On 13 February 1823 the canal clerk was instructed to stop the boats of both companies. On 27 February both iron companies asked the canal company to let them have a copy of their proposed Bill, but were informed that it had 'not yet been drawn', and that a special meeting was to be held on 13 March to rescind the order to apply to Parliament.[104]

Realising that they would get little help from the canal company, the three ironmasters engaged George Overton to plan a tramroad to extend the existing line from Abercynon to Cardiff. Writing to the Powells on 10 August 1823 Overton suggested that he should call at their offices in Brecon on the following Wednesday to discuss the notices to be inserted in the press: he thought that the plans would be ready by the end of the week.[105] The plans, deposited in Cardiff on 29 September, show that the proposed line would cross the river Taff a short way below Abercynon and follow the west bank of the river, very much on the line adopted later for the Taff Vale Railway, to terminate near the White House Bridge in Cardiff – the present Cardiff Bridge is almost on same site – whence it was proposed to make a canal $2\tfrac{1}{4}$ miles long to Cogan House amid the meanders of the Ely river under the shadow of Penarth Head.[106] This rather unpromising terminus was probably chosen by Overton to fit in with a scheme he had propounded to the canal company on 6 June 1821 in an endeavour to get them to finance his plan to unite the mouths of the rivers Taff and Ely to form a large floating harbour.

The canal committee considered the proposed tramroad at their meeting on 4 September 1823, and appointed William Crawshay and his nephew Crawshay Bailey to collate the facts of the case; and on

2 October a sub-committee was appointed to take charge of the company's opposition to the plan.

The tramroad extension died in a rather surprising manner. After several letters had passed between Crawshay and Richard Hill it was revealed to the canal committee on 11 December 1823 that Crawshay had offered to lend each of the three ironmasters £500 of his own shares to enable them to qualify for seats on the committee. A resolution was passed

> ... that the proprietors of the Canal are willing to carry Mr. Crawshay's letter into effect, and that they pledge themselves to elect on their Committee at the next Annual Assembly the three Ironmasters to whom this offer of qualification is addressed, in the event of their accepting it and their abandonment of the projected Tram Road.

A further resolution was passed that within three months of the abandonment of the tramroad the tonnage on iron on the canal would be reduced to 1½d per ton per mile.

These arrangements were ratified at a special canal meeting on 24 January 1824, at which Crawshay and the three ironmasters undertook to advance between them the sum of £15,000 for the improvement of the sea lock at Cardiff. On 26 January the canal solicitor, now William Meyrick of Merthyr, wrote to the Powells of Brecon suggesting a meeting to draft the necessary legal documents,[107] and on 2 June the general meeting elected J. J. Guest of Dowlais, Richard Hill of Plymouth and William Forman of Penydarren to the canal committee, three members of the Crawshay party standing down to make room for them.

The arrangements seem to have worked in a satisfactory manner for a number of years, but the congestion on the canal grew worse with the addition of upward traffic in iron ore in the 1830s, and increased downward traffic in coal. Canal transport was cheap, but from the ironmasters' point of view it was not particularly efficient, and it became more and more obvious that a more rapid and reliable means of reaching the port would have to be found.

Once again it was the ironmasters of Dowlais, Penydarren and Plymouth who set out to find a solution.

Anthony Hill, the younger son of the original Richard Hill, was in charge at the Plymouth works in the early 1830s and had met Isambard Kingdom Brunel in connection with the ironwork required for the Clifton suspension bridge.[108] At the time many people considered that the steam railway was the panacea for all transport problems, and it was natural that the thoughts of the three industrialists should turn in that direction. Hill consulted Brunel, arousing his interest with the result that in November 1834 plans were deposited headed 'Plans for an improved Railway from Merthyr Tydfil to Cardiff', the embryo Taff Vale Railway.[109]

The plans show a railway starting at what later became the Plymouth Street terminus of the Taff Vale Railway in Merthyr (SO 050056) and running south virtually on the line of the present railway. A branch is shown crossing the Merthyr Tramroad at SO 054053, following the line of the later Dowlais Railway to Cae Harris, Dowlais where it was to make an end-on junction with the line from the Dowlais Company's quarries at Castle Morlais. Two branches are shown from this line to Dowlais; one to run northward, parallel with the Merthyr Tramroad to the Penydarren works, and the other running south to serve the Plymouth works. It appears that whoever made the survey mistakenly thought that the Penydarren works obtained its limestone from the same quarries as the Dowlais Company, as there is a branch shown to run from the Dowlais quarry line to the charging bank at Penydarren.

Further plans were deposited on 30 November 1835 showing alterations at the Cardiff end but retaining the same arrangements at Merthyr.[110]

Brunel does not seem to have had a great deal of interest in the TVR, and a note in his diary listing the railways with which he was concerned records 'Merthyr & Cardiff Railway . . . I care not however about it'.[111] He was, however, very prompt in delivering his bill for charges and disbursements which he presented on 20 November 1835, with a request for an early settlement. 'At all events, I have to request that you will be good enough to let me have a check for £500 on account tomorrow, Saturday'.[112]

The TVR obtained its Act (6 & 7 Will 4 c.lxxxii) in 1836, but without powers to make the Dowlais branch, although it was authorised to make a branch in Merthyr to connect with the tramroad. The Act gave the company authority to cross the tramroad made by the Hills to connect their works to the canal basin at Abercanaid on the west of the river, but as there is no mention of crossing the Merthyr Tramroad at any point it must be assumed that it was planned for the railway to run between the tramroad and the river. In 1837 the company obtained another Act

(7 Will 4 & 1 Vict c.lxx) empowering the TVR to continue the branch to Dowlais shown on the deposited plans right into the quarries, and to purchase the tramroad for £21,000. Neither power was exercised.

The three ironworks continued to use the tramroad while the railway was under construction. On 23 July 1839 Anthony Hill, upon whom the responsibility of maintenance of the tramroad rested, wrote to the Dowlais Company as the managers for the current year to complain that, despite repeated applications, he had not received any plates for the tramroad for the past six weeks and that they were now in such short supply that he had had to remove passing places to find sufficient plates to keep the tramroad open. He also complained that

> [t]he Tram Road is nearly impassable. One of the Dowlais engines got off the road by Ynis Owen [ST 076993] about four o'clock P.M. on Saturday last & remained there until mid-day on Monday during which time the whole traffic of the road was obstructed.

He threatened that he would apply to the trustee appointed under the new partnership agreement to use his authority to have locomotives barred from the line, 'which cause the destruction of plates & for the use of which the Tram road was never intended or adapted'.[113]

It is strange that the Merthyr Tramroad never adopted wrought-iron plates. Even after the use of chaired track was adopted the use of 3-foot long cast-iron plates persisted, as did the inconvenience of

30. Site of the canal basin at Abercynon (ST 08479493). Note the pillar designed to support a derrick in front of the central building. The site is now occupied by a fire station. Photo: Gordon Rattenbury (1959)

31 *(below)*. A closer view of the pillar shown above. Note the date '1804'.
Photo from *The Locomotive*, 12 February 1904, reproduced by courtesy of Ian Allan Publishing

32. Stone sleeper block from the Merthyr Tramroad, showing the impression of the tramplate ends and a single spike hole. Blocks of this type were used when the tramroad was first built with the tramplates resting directly on the blocks.
Photo: T. J. Lodge (1973)

33. Double-hole block from the Merthyr Tramroad near Mount Pleasant. Blocks of this type show the use of chaired track which replaced the original track.
Photo: W. E. Howarth (from the RCHS Baxter Tramroad collection) (1946)

* This matter is discussed more fully by Lewis (p.79) in the present work.

regular breakages of the plates under heavy loads. Possibly it was considered more economical to collect the broken rails for re-smelting and re-casting than to invest in the more expensive wrought-iron variety.* Despite the delays due to broken plates it is doubtful if stoppages on the tramroad were as bad as those experienced on the canal between Merthyr and Abercynon with its numerous locks.

The TVR was completed from Cardiff to Abercynon by October 1840 and by April 1841 a single line was in operation from Abercynon to Merthyr. As built the railway crossed the river and the tramroad by a graceful viaduct near Quaker's Yard (FIGS 35, 54) and kept to the east of the tramroad as far as Ynis Owen (ST 077986) where it again crossed the tramroad, this time on the level.

A further Act was obtained in 1840 (3 & 4 Vict c.cx) which renewed the TVR powers to make the branch to Dowlais, but provided that should they start the work but not complete it, the Dowlais Company was to have the right, on giving three months notice, to enter and finish the branch at the expense of the TVR. The TVR made no attempt to start making the branch and their powers were again renewed in 1843 under 7 & 8 Vict c.lxxxiv, which also authorised variations in the route; the rights of the Dowlais Company to complete an unfinished line were retained. In 1848 the TVR constructed a short branch from SO 05350506 in the direction of the branch, but stopped short of crossing the Merthyr to Cardiff turnpike. In 1848, after giving the requisite notice, the Dowlais Company entered the site only to find that the line had not been marked out; before they could start construction the powers of the 1843 Act expired.

It was apparent to the Dowlais Company that they could put no reliance on the TVR, and they applied to Parliament for an Act to make the railway for themselves. But no matter who made the railway to Dowlais, the iron company had to rid themselves of the obligation to carry all their iron on the Merthyr Tramroad imposed by the 1799 and subsequent agreements with the Penydarren and the Plymouth companies.

While their Bill was going through its final stages in Parliament, on 11 July 1849 the Dowlais Company signed an agreement with the two other ironmasters that the latter should purchase Dowlais's five-fourteenths share in the Merthyr Tramroad, and that the land on which the original Dowlais Railroad from Penydarren End to the canal had been laid should be let to the Penydarren Company for 99 years at a peppercorn rent; the Penydarren Company was to maintain it as a tramroad for a minimum of seven years, after which they might surrender their lease if they so wished. Should the tramroad to the canal cease to be used as such the land on which it was laid should revert to the Dowlais Company.[114]

The Dowlais Railway Act received Royal Assent on 18 July 1849. Under its terms the company was authorised to make a railway from the uncompleted works of the TVR near the Merthyr to Cardiff turnpike to a terminus actually in the works site at Dowlais, SO 065075. The iron company was to maintain the junction with the TVR and the existing connection between the railway and the tramroad made under the TVR Act of 1836. Whilst they might start construction, the railway was not to be brought into use until the other partners in the Merthyr Tramroad had agreed to purchase the Dowlais share in that tramroad. The carriage of passengers was permitted, and the other companies were authorised to construct parallel railways if they so wished.

The Dowlais Railway came into use on 21 August 1851.[115] It consisted of a line of 1 mile 72 chains from the TVR at SO 05350506, rising for about 66 chains to SO 061063, in the course of which it climbed some 330ft. Power for the incline was supplied by two twin-cylindered engines supplied by R. & W. Hawthorn which were situated at the latter point.[116] The remaining distance to the works, which climbed a further 40ft, was locomotive-worked.

In 1848 the Dowlais Company's share in the Merthyr Tramroad was valued at £13,439,[117] to purchase which the Penydarren Company had to find £7,466 and the Plymouth £5,973, making their holdings in the tramroad £20,905 (five-ninths) and £16,724 (four-ninths) respectively.

The existing partnership in the Dowlais works was dissolved in 1852, when Sir Josiah J. Guest, as he then was, became sole partner by purchasing the two shares held by the only other partner remaining, E. J. Hutchings, for £58,000. Guest died in November 1852 leaving his whole estate to Lady Charlotte Guest during her widowhood, and in trust for the children of the marriage.[118] George T. Clark was appointed resident trustee of the estate.

The Vale of Neath Railway reached Merthyr on

34. Inclined retaining wall built *c.*1840 to carry the Taff Vale Railway where it adopted a line close to the Merthyr Tramroad between Edwardsville and Mount Pleasant. View facing north. Photo: W. E. Howarth (from the RCHS Baxter Tramroad collection) (1946)

2 November 1853, and in 1854 the Dowlais Extension Railway was authorised as a branch of the Dowlais Railway, leaving that line at Ysgubor Newydd (SO 05600559) to cross the tramroad at SO 05250564 and enter the Vale of Neath goods yard at SO 05230582. Direct interchange was impossible as the Vale of Neath was built to Brunel's broad gauge (7ft 0¼in.). In July 1864 the Vale of Neath laid standard gauge (4ft 8½in.) in addition to the broad gauge enabling Dowlais trains to travel over their lines.

The Penydarren works closed in early 1859, leaving Hill & Co. as the sole users of the Merthyr Tramroad, and the tramroad to the canal fell out of use entirely. It appears that Anthony Hill was apprehensive that the demise of Penydarren would adversely affect his tenure of the tramroad to the quarries. He approached John Williams, the secretary of the embryo Brecon &

Merthyr Railway, who wrote to his company's solicitor, J. R. Cobb (a successor to the Powells of Brecon) on 2 February 1859 advising him that Hill was contemplating putting his limestone traffic onto the B&M, and suggesting that it might be as well to have a specific clause in their Act to cover the point.[119] Ten days later he again wrote to Cobb stating that he thought Hill's traffic would provide the railway with a steady income and that 'At present Mr. Hill's limestone passes along a tramroad through the greater part of the town'.[120]

Whatever enthusiasm Williams and Cobb may have had for Hill's plans was extinguished by a letter to Cobb, also on 12 February, from G. T. Clark pointing out that

> £4,000 will not pay for the outlay Mr. Hill requires even if they are able to cross the ravine at Penydarren which I must doubt unless some Brecon people open their purse strings.[121]

Clark's opinion prevailed with the impecunious B&M, and Hill's pipe-dream faded, leaving his limestone traffic to be carried on the tramroad still.

Anthony Hill died in August 1862, and the Plymouth works and their share in the Merthyr Tramroad were purchased by Richard Fothergill, of the Aberdare ironworks, and a banker, T. A. Hankey, for £250,000 on 12 September 1863. The works continued to smelt iron under the new management, but in 1880 this was given up, and a new company, Hill's Plymouth Co. Ltd, was formed to exploit the collieries attached to the concern.[122] There was now no necessity to maintain a tramroad to the Castle Morlais quarries; and from Penydarren End, where a coal depot was established, to Ynys Owen (ST 087993), where exchange sidings were made with the TVR, the tramroad was altered to a mineral railway. Later a direct connection was made from the TVR to Dyffryn (SO 065030) and the mineral railway was cut off at a little to the north of Troedyrhiw (SO 073025). A further connection was made into the Vale of Neath goods yard at Merthyr which was entered at SO 05220565, a little to the west of the point at which the Dowlais Extension Railway entered.

In 1888 the lease to the Dowlais Company of Gwaunfarren Farm, including the land over which the tramroad from Penydarren to Castle Morlais passed, was surrendered by the iron company, and presumably there was no further use made of the tramroad.[123]

35. The Taff Vale viaduct at Quaker's Yard (ST 089965) was originally opened in 1841. It was widened in 1862 when this photograph was taken by Joseph Collings of Cardiff. It shows clearly that the Merthyr Tramroad was still in use at this date. Note that the horse path is made up to the level of the running surface of the plates and the sleeper blocks cannot be seen. Photo: John Minnis collection

Merthyr Tydfil Tramroads

The Locomotives

BY
M. J. T. LEWIS

Introduction

THE Merthyr Tramroad is famed above all else as the line on which in 1804, for the first time in history, a locomotive indisputably hauled a load on a railway – I say 'indisputably' because clouds of uncertainty surround the Coalbrookdale engine of 1802–3. Trevithick's locomotive was followed, after a pause of 25 years, by a number more – many of them Welsh-built by Neath Abbey Ironworks – which traversed the Merthyr Tramroad and connecting lines. All these formed the subject of a paper I wrote nearly 30 years ago.[124] In this new edition, I have reduced the introductory matter, which partly duplicated the first part of the present book, to a mere summary of the complex story behind the tramroads under review. I have corrected the errors of which I am aware and incorporated more recent findings. And I have added a completely new section on Cyfarthfa, which fell outside my original brief, and the hitherto unknown locomotives there. This book is about tramroads. I therefore deal only with those locomotives that ran, or could run, on plateways. Later arrivals designed only for edge rails are another story.

The drawings and descriptions of the engines derive from four major sources, to whose custodians I offer my thanks for permission to re-draw or quote from them. Those of *Eclipse* rely on the Robert Stephenson & Co. collection, now divided between the Science Museum Library and the National Railway Museum at York. For the engines built by Neath Abbey Ironworks the main written source is the Dowlais Iron Company in-letters (numbering well over half a million) deposited by Guest Keen Iron & Steel Co. Ltd in the Glamorgan Record Office in Cardiff.[125] While Neath Abbey's in-letters do not survive, the invaluable collection of its drawings does. Originally deposited at Cardiff by Taylor & Sons of Briton Ferry, it is now at the West Glamorgan Record Office in Swansea. Finally the tantalising evidence for Cyfarthfa engines is in the Cyfarthfa collection (essentially Crawshay family correspondence) in the National Library of Wales at Aberystwyth.

In the first edition I acknowledged the unstinted help of Gordon Rattenbury, Les Charlton, Richard Keen and Francis Parker. To their names I now gratefully add those of Dr David Gwyn, Jim Rees and Dr John van Laun, who have read drafts and freely shared their insights and information. I also thank John Liffen for much guidance, and Roger Kidner for discussing the Cyfarthfa locomotives. For the cover of this book, Michael Blackmore has recreated *Perseverance* with his incomparable artistry and technical understanding. Above all I am indebted to Dr Michael Bailey for sparing no effort in keeping me on the right track in the surprisingly numerous matters relating to Robert Stephenson & Co. and the Liverpool & Manchester Railway, and to Paul Reynolds for his constant supply of information, criticism and editorial support.

Finally, plans are afoot to build a working reconstruction, as authentic as modern requirements permit, of the Dowlais locomotive *Perseverance*. There are a host of obstacles, not least financial, to be surmounted; but one day, it is hoped, that unique sight will once again grace the Merthyr Tydfil scene.

M. J. T. L

The Tramroads

THE four ironworks at Merthyr Tydfil grew rapidly in the early nineteenth century. By 1845 Dowlais was the largest ironworks in the world, employing a workforce of 7,300. Cyfarthfa, which had long been ahead of it, was now not far behind, while Penydarren and Plymouth were smaller. All mined or quarried their own ore, coal and limestone, and all had their own complex of railway systems within the works and linking the works to the pits and quarries and to the canal. Most of the lines first laid in the 1790s were originally edge railways (or 'railroads' in standard south Wales parlance) laid with cast-iron bar rails, but around 1800 nearly all were converted into plateways ('tramroads'[126]) and thereafter, until the 1830s and sometimes even later, new lines were built as plateways.

At the turn of the century the standard plate rail was of Benjamin Outram's favoured type: cast-iron, 3ft long, and spiked down through a notch in the end into wooden plugs in holes in stone blocks (FIG. 36, A), although the cast-iron sill or cross-tie was already coming into use (FIG. 36, B). Later, individual chairs appeared (FIG. 36, C), associated especially with rolled wrought-iron plates and with locomotive working.[127]

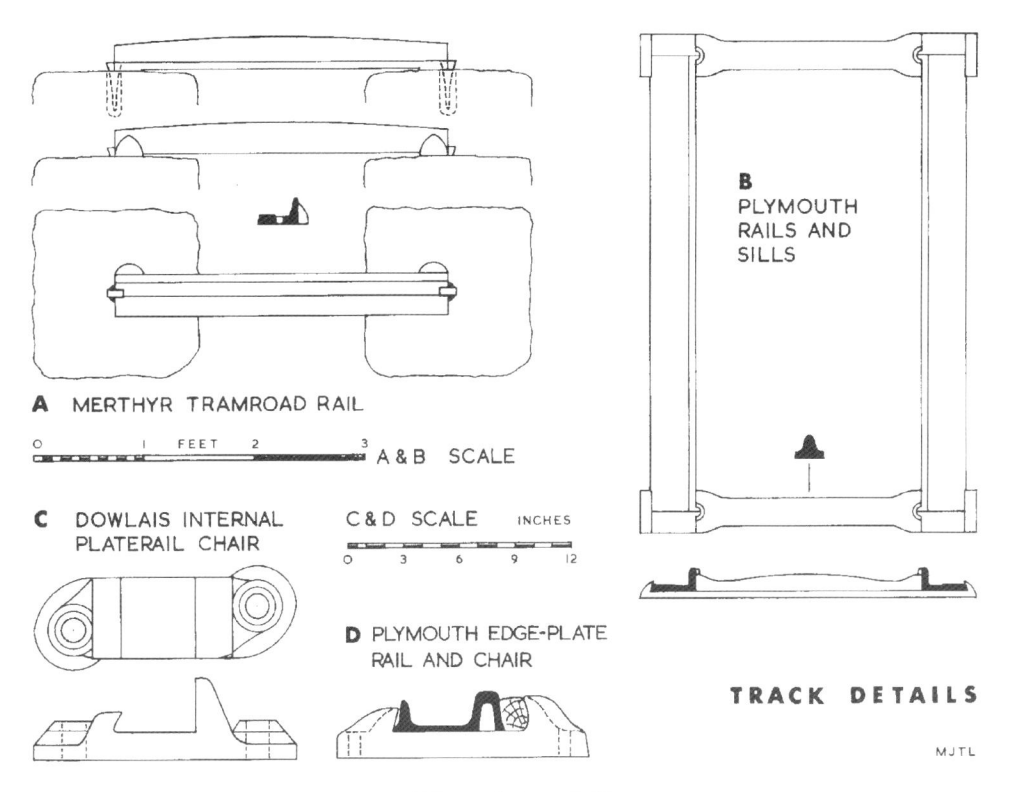

36. Plates, chairs and sills.

37. The southern portal of the tunnel at Plymouth ironworks (SO 057046), restored in the 1990s as 'Trevithick's tunnel'. The tunnel itself remains buried.
Photo: Jonathan Reynolds (2003)

Around Merthyr there was a bewildering variety of gauges, and a word is desirable about how they are measured. The most common practice nowadays is to quote the gauge *between* the flanges, which in operational terms is largely meaningless. What matters is the gauge measured *over* the flanges – **the figure which, unless otherwise stated, will be given hereafter** – because it is this which dictates the gauge between the wheels. In practice, some play was allowed and the wheel gauge was greater still. As a rough rule of thumb, these three measurements increase in steps of two inches. Thus the Merthyr Tramroad gauge was 4ft 2in. between the flanges, 4ft 4in. over them, and approximately 4ft 6in. between the wheels. But exactitude was less important than with edge rails, and it was not unknown for plateways to acquire a middle-age spread.

The bare details of the relevant tramroads from 1802 when the Merthyr Tramroad opened are:

1. The Merthyr Tramroad itself ran for 9½ miles from a junction with the Dowlais Tramroad at Penydarren End to the canal basin at Abercynon. It was single-track with frequent passing loops and plates of standard Outram type weighing about 60lb. At Plymouth works the line passed underneath the furnace charging area in a tunnel 40 yards long, 8ft high and 8ft wide,[128] ample clearance for horse-drawn trams but a distinct impediment to locomotive working (FIG.37). The overall gradient is about 1 in 145. According to George Overton, who engineered the tramroad, it varied from 1 in 396 to 1 in 132 with 'some parts' at 1 in 36 or steeper.[129] Others give the maximum gradient as 1 in 109 or as 1 in 50.[130]

The traffic consisted largely of iron for export from Cardiff, and grew markedly for the first 40 years of the tramroad's life. The ironworks' output in tons was as follows (including, for comparison's sake, Cyfarthfa's, although it did not use the tramroad):[131]

	1805	1820	1830	1840
Cyfartha	10,460	19,010	19,892	35,507
Dowlais	6,800	11,115	27,647	45,218
Penydarren	7,803	8,690	11,744	16,130
Plymouth	5,789	7,941	12,177	12,922

An ever-increasing proportion of the pig-iron from the furnaces was puddled and rolled into wrought-iron bars, which by 1830 formed the great majority of the exports. From the late 1820s more and more iron ore was imported, a traffic which, outstripping the tramroad's capacity on the uphill haul, was largely carried by canal up to Merthyr and there transferred (if destined for Penydarren or Dowlais) to the Penydarren Company's tramroad. In 1835, for example, Dowlais alone imported 15,668 tons of ore and cinders.

About the trams which carried this traffic, remarkably little is known. For bulk cargoes such as iron ore they probably resembled those preferred by George Overton himself

> . . . which are constructed with sides one foot upright, and nine inches upon that, to bevel a little outwards. The sides consist of four elm planks, two on each side, the lower planks two inches thick, the upper ones an inch and a half, with straps of iron under the bottom, extending to the top edge of the sides, which were screwed together, with inch elm boards on the bottom.

38 *(right)*. Dowlais furnace tops, 1840. Note the tram in the foreground. Watercolour: George Childs, reproduced by permission of the National Museums & Galleries of Wales

39 *(below)*. Penydarren ironworks in 1813. Note bar-iron trams bottom right of picture. From J. G. Wood, *The Principal Rivers of Wales Illustrated*

This description of tram I introduced more than twenty-four years ago [that is, before 1801] and it has since been adopted at most of the works throughout South Wales.[132]

Mercer thought such trams were about 7ft 6in. long by 4ft 9in. wide at the top, with a tare weight of 15cwt and cast-iron wheels about 2ft 6in. in diameter. Their capacity was about two tons, and trams of this design survived at Penydarren until its closure in 1859.[133] For carrying the ubiquitous bar iron there were perhaps two kinds of vehicle. For shorter bars there were long-wheel-base four-wheeled trucks, as in Wood's view of Penydarren in 1813 (FIG.39); for long bars there were bolsters connected in pairs, apparently by long draw-bars, to form simple bogie trucks as seen in Thomas Hornor's view of Penydarren in 1817.[134] Quite possibly these were in use on the Merthyr Tramroad as early as 1803 when 'two waggons coupled together and loaded with ten tons of bar iron are comfortably hauled by one horse'.[135] Later three horses hauled a train of 25 tons,[136] and ultimately, to deal with the rapidly-growing traffic, locomotives were introduced. Trevithick's engine of 1804 was no more than an experiment which was only a partial success. Regular locomotive working began in 1832, with one engine owned by the Penydarren Company and several by Dowlais. Passenger traffic, though quite unofficial, was winked at and anyone willing to tip the driver was allowed to perch on the bar iron.

2. Below the new junction with the Merthyr Tramroad, the old Dowlais Railroad from the works to the canal was apparently abandoned in 1802; but above the junction, to permit through running from Dowlais to Abercynon, it was converted to 4ft 4in. plateway. The land is steep here. Dowlais stands at over 1,000ft, almost 500ft above the Taff at Merthyr, and this upper section was very heavily graded – an average of

about 1 in 23, with a maximum of 1 in 16½ – and from 1832 was worked by rack locomotives.

3. The Penydarren Company's tramroad to the canal at Merthyr remained in place. Its gauge is uncertain but was narrow: most likely 2ft 6in., the same as the Morlais quarry tramroad which was more or less contemporary. For a time it was probably little used except when the Merthyr Tramroad was obstructed. But about 1827 it was converted to 4ft 4in. gauge to allow the new iron-ore traffic from the canal to run through to Dowlais, and the Bethesda Street tunnel was bypassed. Gordon Rattenbury thought the reason was to permit locomotive working. The tunnel's width of 9ft 6in.,[137] however, is ample and if its minimum headroom (currently 11ft) was inadequate it would surely have been easier to provide a locomotive with a lowering chimney than re-route a substantial length of tramroad. In any event the average gradient of about 1 in 33 against the load (for iron ore) seems excessive for locomotive working at that date.

4. Limestone for Dowlais came from Twynau Gwynion quarries along a plateway built by George Overton about 1800 with a gauge of 2ft 8in.,[138] which was certainly never locomotive-worked. But in 1825 Dowlais was hounded out by the landowner and turned instead to the eastern Morlais quarries. Carts must have been used for transport until in 1833–4 the 'New Limestone Railroad' was built for the substantial sum of £4,372.[139] A number of facts cast doubt on the usual assumption that this was a plateway. In 1832 Dowlais had already taken delivery of a locomotive (*Yn Barod Etto*) with dual-purpose wheels for running on either standard-gauge edge rails or 4ft 4in.-gauge plate rails. In 1834 the first plans for the proposed Taff Vale Railway envisaged a branch to Dowlais and an end-on junction there with the Morlais line. In 1835 Dowlais bought its first purely standard-gauge locomotive. Large stone blocks for chaired edge rail survive on the route. Although certainty is impossible, all these facts taken together suggest that the Morlais–Dowlais line was not only an edge railway – the normal meaning of 'railroad' – but a standard-gauge one intended for locomotives from the start. The gradient, averaging 1 in 160, was gentle enough.

5. The tramroad carrying limestone from the western Morlais quarries to Penydarren works was of 2ft 6in. gauge, but in 1803 a third rail was added to allow through carriage on the 4ft 4in. gauge from the quarries to Plymouth works as well.[140] It was part of the 'General Road' of the Merthyr Tramroad, maintained by the three participating ironworks. Penydarren's *Eclipse*, as converted in 1832, could in theory have run to Morlais, but the overall gradient of 1 in 30, though with the load, makes this improbable.

6. Inside Dowlais works and serving the various coal and ironstone mines to east and south was a network of tramroads, some (like that from the Nantyglo and Four Foot levels) converted from railroads by Overton about 1800,[141] some built later. Totalling by the 1840s well over 100 miles, they were partly on 4ft 4in. gauge and partly on the Dowlais gauge of 2ft 8in., and latterly their rails sat in iron sills or heavy chairs. By about 1840, when another long route was built to Cwmbargoed, standard gauge had been introduced. Most of the mines lay considerably higher than the works, to which they were connected by inclines. The internal system, and probably the relatively level parts of the major coal lines, came to be locomotive-worked.

7. Penydarren works had a similar but smaller complex of tramroads internally and from the mines. One gauge here – we do not know exactly where – was apparently 3ft, for which the company's only locomotive was built. Another ('Homfray's old dram road') was 2ft 4½in.,[142] although it is not clear whether this was compatible with the 2ft 6in. Morlais gauge.

8. Plymouth works was easily served by the Merthyr Tramroad, which ran through it. In 1807 its new Pentrebach forge was connected to the tramroad by a steep branch and to the Plymouth furnaces by a line which in 1820 was extended to Dyffryn furnaces. By 1822 if not before, this system had plates laid in cast-iron sills,[143] partly on 2ft 2in. gauge, partly on 4ft 4in. It had no early locomotives.

9. Cyfarthfa works, on the other side of the river and canal, was alone in not being connected to the Merthyr Tramroad system. It too had its own tramroads, as well as its own canal, to coal and ore pits and from 1814 to its new furnaces at Ynysfach to the south. More relevant, it had the old railroad from its limestone quarries at Gurnos which at some date unknown was converted to a plateway of almost 3ft gauge between the flanges or 3ft 1in. over them and which in 1830–1 was rebuilt for locomotive working. Its gradient was of the order of 1 in 80.

Penydarren Company Locomotives

Trevithick's Locomotive

THE outline of the story of the famous Penydarren locomotive is clear enough, but no new information of significance has emerged for decades and the many uncertain details have been debated almost *ad nauseam*. Few fresh insights can be offered here.

Richard Trevithick built his first railway locomotive in 1802–3 for the Coalbrookdale Company, the first firm to take an interest in his high-pressure engine after the patent of 1802, but there is no evidence that it ever ran under its own power. He next interested Samuel Homfray and built several stationary engines for Penydarren ironworks. The background to the building of the locomotive at Penydarren was a wager of 500 guineas made by Homfray with Richard Crawshay of Cyfarthfa that he would haul, by the power of steam, a load of ten tons of iron from Penydarren to Abercynon and the empties back. Richard Hill of Plymouth held the stakes. On 1 October 1803 Trevithick wrote to his patron Davies Giddy:

> There will be a realroad engine at work here in a fortnight; it will go on reals not exceeding an elevation of one-fiftieth part of a perpendicular [presumably meaning 1 in 50] and of considerable length. The cylinder is 8½ in diameter, to go about two and a half miles an hour; it is to have the same velocity of the piston rod. It will weigh, water and all complete, within 5 tons.[144]

He was over-optimistic, for he was diverted to other work and no more is heard until 15 February 1804:

> Last saturday [11 February] we lighted the fire in the Tram Waggon and work'd it without the wheels to try the engine; on Monday we put it on the Tram Road. It work'd very well, and ran up hill and down with great ease, and very managable. We have plenty of steam and power.

This trip, on 13 February 1804, was the first recorded run by a railway locomotive. On 20 February Trevithick reported:

> The Tram Waggon have been at work several times. It works exceeding well, and is much more managable than horses. We have not try'd to draw but ten tons at a time yet, but I dought not but we cou'd draw 40 tons at a time very well for 10 tons stands no chance at all with it. We have not been but two miles on the road and back again, and shall not go further untill Mr Homfray comes home . . . The engine, with water enclued, is ab't 5 tons. It runs up the Tram road of 2 Inch in a Yard [1 in 18, presumably on the Dowlais section] 40 stroakes pr min't with the empty waggons. The engine moves forth 9 feet every stroake. The publick is much taken up with it. The bet of 5 Hund'd Guineas will be desided abt the end of this Week . . . The steam thats disscharged from the engine is turned up the chimney abt 3 feet above the fire, and when the engine is working 40 St pr mt [strokes per minute], 4½ ft Stroake, Cylinder 8¼ In Diam, not the smallest particle of steam appears out of the top of the chimny, tho' the Chimny is but 8 feet above where the steam is delivered into it . . . The fire burns much better when the steam goes up the Chimney that what it do when the engine is Idle. I intend to make a smaller engine for the road, as this has much moore power than is wanted here. This engine is to work a hammer.

The trip to decide the bet was made on 21 February. Trevithick wrote next day:

> Yesterday we proceeded on our journey with the engine; we carry'd ten tons of Iron, five waggons, and 70 Men riding on them the whole of the journey. Its above 9 miles which we perform'd in

4 hours & 5 mints, but we had to cut down som trees and remove some Large rocks out of the road. The engine, while working, went nearly 5 miles pr hour, there was no water put into the boiler from the time we started untill we arriv'd at our journey's end. The coal consumed was 2 Hund[d]. On our return home, abt 4 miles from the shipping place of the Iron, one of the small bolts that fastened the axel to the boiler broak, and let all the water out of the boiler, which prevented the engine returning untill this evening.

Homfray was delighted. The engine, he said, 'goes very easy 4 miles per hour and is as trackable as a horse, will *back* its load and move it forward as little (and slow) at a time as you please.' Hill, however, proved to be a hair-splitter. He refused to pay up because, Trevithick lamented, 'there were some of the tram-plates that was in the tunnel removed so as to get the road in the middle of the arch ... his objection is that the road is not in the same place as when the bet was made.' His next niggle was that the engine did not return the empty trams in the same time as horses usually did because the force pump could not fill the boiler, which had to be refilled with cold water. Whether the bet was ever honoured we do not know.

The engine ran several times more. On 4 March Trevithick reported that he had tried it with 25 tons of iron, for which it was more than a match. On another trip on 24 March the engine, heavily ballasted, broke many plates. On 13 April Homfray confirmed that the engine, now pumping water, had a cast-iron return-flue boiler 6ft by 4ft 3in. and a cylinder 8in. by 4ft 6in.[145] Before early July it hauled at least two more trains, but thereafter seems to have run no more on rails. There are various versions of its latter days: driving a hammer at Penydarren, winding at Penydarren coal pits, working an incline at Cwmbargoed, winding at Cyfarthfa, or a combination of these functions. In this guise it may have survived into the 1850s.

This is the sum of the useful contemporary evidence, from which we can be sure of several things. There was a single cylinder 8¼in. by 54in., which must have been horizontal: if vertical, the end of the piston rod at the top of the stroke would be a good 9ft above the base of the cylinder, and Plymouth tunnel was only 8ft high. The cast-iron boiler was 4ft 3in. by 6ft and there was a feed-water heater. The chimney stood about 11ft high above the firebox,

and must have been detachable to pass the tunnel, where the track was moved probably to allow the flywheel to fit. Though there is no direct evidence for the flywheel, it is difficult to imagine that there was not one. The exhaust was turned into the chimney where Trevithick found that it helped the fire to draw. The engine weighed about 5 tons in working order, and travelled at 4 to 5mph. The statements that 'the engine moves forth 9ft every stroake' and 'it is to have the same velocity of the piston rod' mean the same, namely that it advanced 4ft 6in. for each single 4ft 6in. stroke of the piston or 9ft per return stroke. At 40 return strokes a minute, this makes a little over 4mph. If the gear ratio was 1 to 1, the wheel diameter was rather over 2ft 10in. Geared it must have been, in view of the enormous stroke. The engine could be put to non-railway work without its wheels.

There is a fair amount of secondary evidence – early technical books purporting to describe the locomotive, and memories of local people recorded mainly in the 1850s. This information is not entirely to be trusted. Some is blatantly untrue: that there were two cylinders, that the cylinder was vertical (and of different dimensions from those Trevithick gave), that the wheels were driven directly, that the engine had a brick chimney (a persistent local legend, this), that the boiler was wrought-iron, that the engine made only one trip. Some stories may conceivably be true (that the engine was banished from the tramroad because it broke both axles); some are very likely true (that the chimney was of plate iron, that the tube to it was about 14in. in diameter, that William Richards was the driver).[146] The recollections of Rees Jones, recorded in 1858, are more trustworthy than many, allowing for the fading memory of an 82-year-old. He got some details wrong, but confirmed others. He was overlooker of the Penydarren engines in 1804, and said that most or all of the engineering was done at Penydarren, the fitting by himself, the boiler and smithwork by Richard Brown. This should probably be William Brown whom Francis Trevithick knew as 'my Father's right-hand man in making the engine'[147] and who in 1830, now proprietor of Blaina ironworks, built a locomotive for himself. The engine was first used, Jones said, to bring iron from the furnaces to the forge, where it worked well but broke many plates and couplings. It then hauled iron down to Abercynon, again breaking many plates. The pressure was about 40psi and steam distribution was by a typical Trevithick four-way rotary cock.

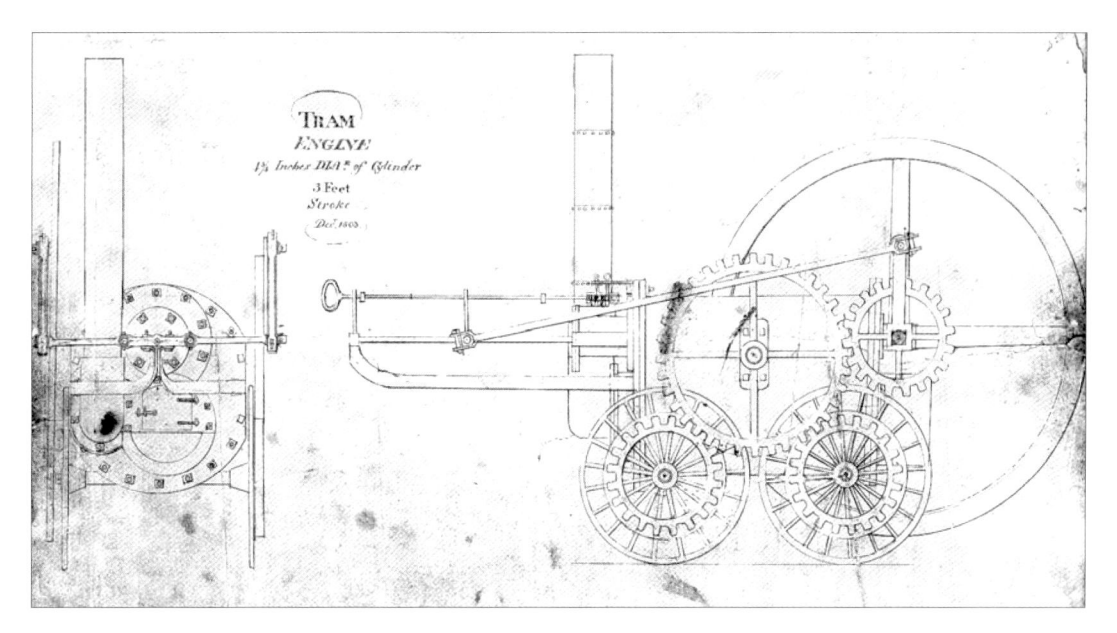

40. John Llewellyn's drawing of Trevithick's 3-foot gauge locomotive.
Reproduced by permission of the Science Museum/Science & Society Picture Library

There remains the famous drawing (FIG.40) made by John Llewellyn who worked with Trevithick at Merthyr.[148] It is a pricked copy of an earlier drawing, a little crudely done, and it came to the Patent Office Museum (now the Science Museum) in 1862 via Llewellyn's nephew and William Menelaus, the Dowlais manager. It shows a plateway locomotive with cast-iron return-flue boiler (the box on the boiler back probably connected two separate flue tubes, in place of a single bent tube), a horizontal cylinder mostly enclosed in the boiler, return connecting rods from the cross-head to a crankshaft with a large flywheel, and a 1 to 1 geared drive to the wheels on one side. It has a rotary steam valve and wheels loose on the axles. The legend reads: 'Tram Engine 4¾ Inches Dia^R of Cylinder 3 Feet Stroke Decr 1803'. There is no other scale. This drawing is still frequently taken to represent the engine that first ran on 13 February 1804, and as such has been copied, miscopied, described, misdescribed and imaginatively interpreted on countless occasions.

As has been pointed out several times in the past, however, this simply cannot be the case. The cylinder dimensions given in the legend are much too small. Moreover, by using the throw of the crank (1ft 6in.) as a measure, the gauge of the wheels scales at about 3ft 1½in., not the 4ft 6in. required for the Merthyr Tramroad. It has been suggested that it is a copy (size for size, because it is pricked off) of a drawing of the original engine, but with the scale altered to give a general idea of the smaller locomotive that Trevithick said he intended to build in his letter of 20 February.[149] Another suggestion is that the legend is false, added considerably later when the true scale had been forgotten.[150] In both cases, the theory is that the original legend or scale gave the stroke as 4ft 6in. These two ideas can be dealt with together. Firstly, the style of the legend is entirely appropriate to 1803. Second, if the stroke were 4ft 6in., the gauge would be about 4ft 6in., which fits perfectly, and the boiler would be about the right size; but not one of the other dimensions agrees with contemporary statements. The chimney, for instance, is much too short; the flywheel is far too high for the tunnel; and the distance travelled per return stroke would be 14ft, not 9ft. Lastly, if the stroke is 4ft 6in., the scale of the drawing is ⅔ inch to the foot, a curious one; if the stroke is 3ft as the legend says, the scale is the eminently reasonable one of 1 inch to the foot. There seems no room for doubt. This is not the famous Penydarren engine, but a 3ft-gauge one.

What then is it? It is certainly a Trevithick design – there are no other candidates – and equally certainly the Penydarren engine bore a family resemblance to

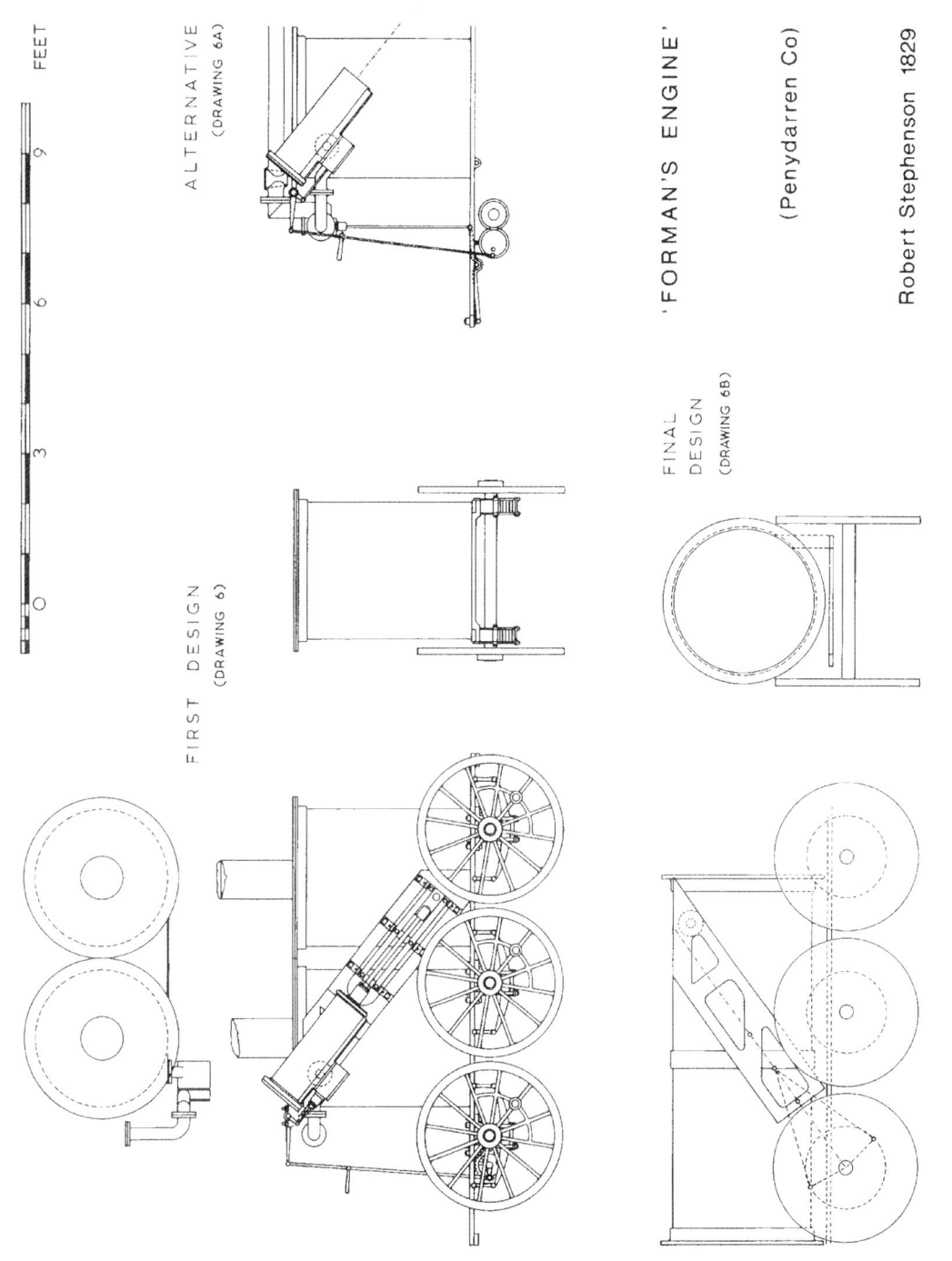

Merthyr Tydfil Tramroads and their Locomotives

41. 'Forman's engine', Robert Stephenson 1829.

it, though the details clearly differed. Two possible claimants present themselves. One is a hypothetical engine for the internal 3ft-gauge system which Penydarren seems, at least later, to have had. But the smaller engine which Trevithick planned in his letter of 20 February was intended for the Merthyr tramroad ('the road'), and there is no suggestion that a narrower-gauge engine was ever contemplated, let alone built. The much more probable claimant is the Coalbrookdale engine. Here we have a little more to go on. One of the plateway gauges in that district was 3ft (notably the main line from the Dale to the Severn wharf); Trevithick refers to one of his Coalbrookdale engines, possibly the locomotive, as having a cylinder 5in. by 3ft; and the locomotive cylinder is said to have survived until 1884 when a casual visitor describes it as 4in. by about 3ft, figures which agree roughly with those on the drawing.[151] On this interpretation, the drawing may have been made to show Homfray the kind of engine he was going to get.

It is not likely that Homfray envisaged Trevithick's locomotive as a permanent replacement for horses in hauling Penydarren iron. Both he and Trevithick regarded it as an experimental multi-purpose machine which, by pumping, winding, powering a hammer, and hauling iron on rails would demonstrate the compactness, power and versatility of the new high-pressure engine. In any event, it proved the point which later became increasingly obvious, that cast-iron rails and locomotives did not go well together. Wrought-iron rail was an essential prerequisite for the full development of the railway engine. Plates broke aplenty under the loaded trams with a maximum gross weight of 3 tons; many more broke under the 5 tons of the engine. Davies Giddy wrote at the time that because of these breakages 'on the whole the Experiment was considered as a failure'. But at least it showed the way forward and proved that steam power could haul useful loads on rails by simple adhesion. Although it took nearly a decade for Trevithick's message to be more widely heeded, already in March 1804 the promoters of the Oystermouth Railway at Swansea were contemplating the possibility of steam traction.[152]

The Stephenson Locomotive

For 25 years after 1804 south Wales knew no locomotives, apart from two unconfirmed trials (a Blenkinsop engine at Nantyglo about 1813 and one by William Stewart on the Monmouthshire Canal Company's tramroads in 1816) and the more substantial use of a George Stephenson locomotive at Llansamlet near Swansea in 1819.[153] Then suddenly in the late 1820s, in line with the quickening pace of locomotive development in the North East, south Wales too began to take a serious interest. In 1828 two engines were ordered from Robert Stephenson & Co. of Newcastle. One, known to Stephensons only as 'Forman's Engine' or 'No.14 Travelling Engine', was ordered early in December by William Forman, by now senior partner in Penydarren ironworks. Thompson, Forman & Son (that is, Penydarren) had since 1826 been one of the main suppliers of pig-iron to Robert Stephenson & Co.[154] The other ('Homfray's Engine', 'No.15 Travelling Engine' or, later, *Britannia*) was ordered quite separately and later in the month by Samuel Homfray of Tredegar, son of Trevithick's patron, for hauling trains on the 4ft 4in.-gauge Sirhowy Tramroad.[155]

The original plans for Forman's engine (FIG.41),[156] undated but attributable to late 1828 or early 1829, show an 0-6-0 with twin vertical boilers after the fashion of *Twin Sisters* then being built for the Liverpool & Manchester. It was to have plateway wheels 3ft in diameter and set 3ft 1½in. apart for running on rails of 3ft gauge, steeply inclined cylinders (an arrangement recently inaugurated on Stephenson's *Lancashire Witch*), and valve motion driven via crank and rocker arms by a gear wheel on the rear axle. But the design was drastically changed, for an outline drawing dated July 1829 shows a horizontal boiler. According to another source the flue, probably a single non-return one, was elliptical in section, perhaps to increase the heating surface and to minimise distortion fractures due to expansion.[157] As was normal with Stephenson engines of this date, the boiler plates, $5/16$in. thick, were brought in from J. & W. Bennitt of Dudley.[158] The inclined cylinders, 7in. by 20in., were mounted on the boiler back, the frames were of flat bar 3in. by 1in., and the wheels were 3ft. This engine, stripped down to its components for reassembly on arrival, was shipped from Newcastle in July 1829, together with *Britannia*, to the Tredegar Iron Company's Pillgwenlly wharf at Newport whence it was presumably taken on to Penydarren by road. It cost £375 plus £19-odd for freight, packing and extras.[159]

For two years or so it hauled trams on, one supposes, the internal works system, for the Merthyr Tramroad and the lines to Morlais quarry and (probably) to the canal were of different gauge. There is,

Merthyr Tydfil Tramroads and their Locomotives

ECLIPSE
Robert Stephenson 1829
as rebuilt 1832

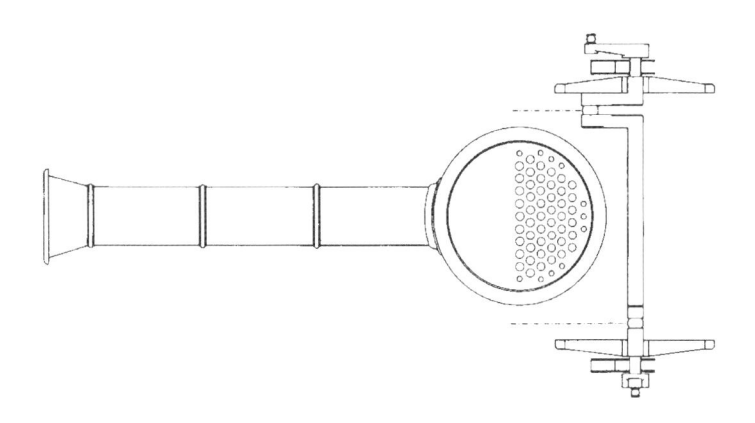

FEET
0　3　6　9　12

42. *Eclipse*, as rebuilt by Robert Stephenson 1832.

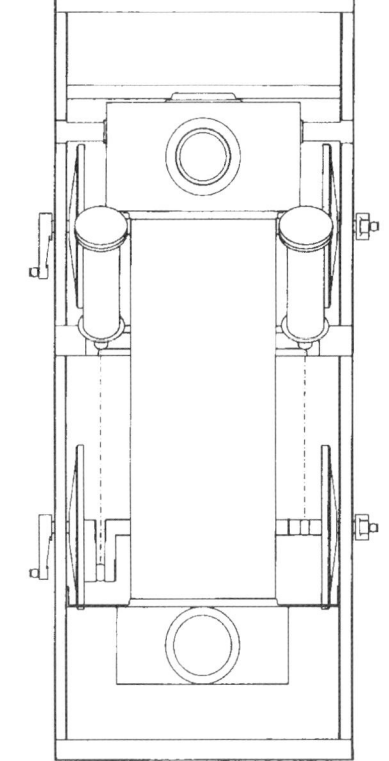

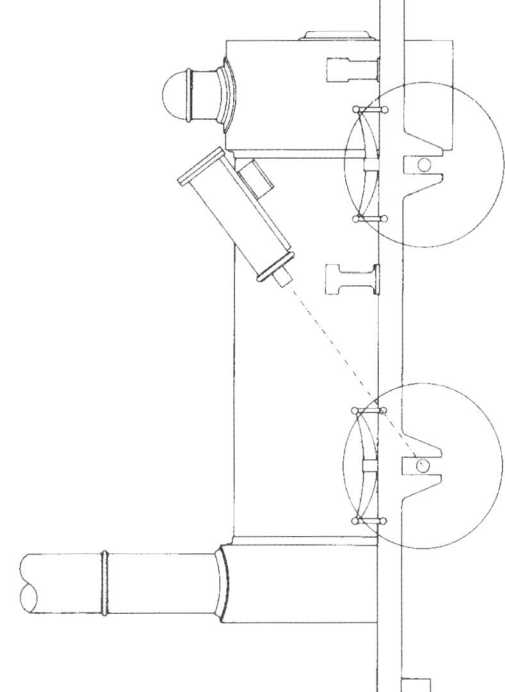

however, an awkwardness. William Forman being in charge of Penydarren, it is always assumed that the locomotive was built for Penydarren. Yet there is currently no other evidence for a 3ft gauge there. At the time, Forman was also senior partner at Rhymney which included the new Bute ironworks. One therefore wonders if Formans's engine was actually intended for Bute's limestone tramroad to Twynau Gwynion, which was built on a gauge of 2ft 11½in. or 3ft at just the right time (1826–7) and was certainly locomotive-worked at a later date.[160] This could explain why Forman's engine was delivered to Newport (convenient for Bute) rather than Cardiff (convenient for Penydarren). The difficulty is that the limestone tramroad gradients, up to 1 in 30, seem impossibly heavy for a locomotive of 1829. That Forman's engine did work at Penydarren therefore remains probable, but it is not a certainty.

It is certain, however, that it was at Penydarren from 1832, when it was returned to Stephensons for conversion to the Merthyr Tramroad gauge plus 2in. play, making 4ft 6in. (FIG.42).[161] The boiler shell (2ft 9in. by 7ft 2½in.) was probably retained, but it was given 82 copper tubes, a smokebox and a vaulted firebox with dome on top; the heating surface now totalled 289.75sq.ft.[162] The cylinders remained in the same place, but new axles were needed with the cranks inside the wheels, and a new sandwich frame, typical of current Stephenson practice, was fitted outside the wheels. The arrangement was altered to 0-4-0, with new wheels of 3ft 6in. diameter.[163] The chimney stood 12ft 7in. high above rail level, and although the drawing shows it fixed, it must have been lowerable to pass through Plymouth tunnel. The engine that resulted from this metamorphosis was not unlike the standard four-coupled Stephenson *Samson* type of the time, except for the external inclined cylinders (by then old-fashioned) and the unusual crank axle arrangement.

In this new guise the engine began to work on the Merthyr Tramroad on 22 June 1832. *The Cambrian* for 30 June described the occasion:

> On Friday last a new Locomotive Engine, called the Eclipse, started from the Penydarran Iron Works, Merthyr Tydfil, with a load of 23 tons of bar and rod iron, which was delivered at the basin of the Glamorganshire Canal, 10 miles from the works, in one hour and forty-eight minutes. – The engine then returned with the empty carriages, crowded with passengers, whom the novelty of the occasion had attracted, and reached the works, in one hour and 45 minutes, from the time of its leaving the basin, including all stoppages on the road for water, &c. – This was performed twice in the course of the day, and had there been occasion, it could have made another trip with the greatest ease. The day following it came up from the same point, drawing the same number of carriages, and conveying 145 passengers, in one hour and 14 minutes, including stoppages; and as preparations are making to obviate the necessity of taking in water on the road, it is expected that the journey will be accomplished in future easily and safely in an hour. This engine was built at Newcastle-upon-Tyne, by Messrs Robert Stephenson, and Co. the celebrated locomotive Engine-builders, who have made those engines now travelling on the Liverpool and Manchester Railway; it has been much admired for the symmetry of its proportions, and being very low and compact in general appearance, conveys to the mind a pleasing idea of smugness and aptitude for the task assigned to it. The means of generating steam is so abundant that it was blowing off at the safety valve nearly the whole length of the journey forward and back, and the appearance of the engine altogether puts one strongly in mind of one of those low built craft, which although buried in the spray, and scarcely appearing above the water, yet sweep through it with the ease and swiftness of a Dolphin. It has two 7-inch steam cylinders of 20 inches stroke, is mounted on four wheels 3 feet 4 inches in diameter, and weighs, when the boiler is charged with water, and in working trim, about five tons.

How long *Eclipse* lasted is quite unknown. It is unlikely to have worked the tramroad to Morlais (west), for although it would now fit the gauge the gradients were steep. History tells of it no more, which may mean that, despite its apparent success, it proved too light for the heavy work required.[164]

Cyfarthfa Ironworks Locomotives

Hirwaun

EARLY locomotives certainly existed at the Crawshays' Cyfarthfa works, but the evidence is sadly fragmentary. It will be best first to clear out of the way the complicating issue of the locomotive at the Crawshays' other ironworks at Hirwaun. William Crawshay I presided dictatorially over his disunited family from London, while his son William II was in charge of operations in Wales. William II, much to the disapproval of his penny-pinching father, was an enthusiast for steam traction. In March 1830 he persuaded Goldsworthy Gurney, the pioneer of road locomotives, to bring to Wales one of his patent drags or road tractors with water-tube boiler and horizontal inside cylinders (FIG.43). This was fitted with plateway wheels and tested first on a specially-laid track at Cyfarthfa and then on the existing 4ft 4in. tramroad at Hirwaun, with highly satisfactory results. That was merely an experiment. But in July 1830 William II bought an engine from Gurney, possibly built specifically for railway use, which worked at Hirwaun until at least February 1832 when he described in detail the work it had done throughout the calendar year 1831. It had then been in continuous use there for 18 months.[165]

William II's son Francis recalled in old age that Gurney's engine did so well that Welsh mechanics 'broke up all their old engines and substituted new locomotives in their place'; but this probably reflects the rapid development after 1830 of locomotives in general, not in any specific place.[166] There is no evidence that, until much later, there was more than the one locomotive at Hirwaun. Its story is relatively full and clear but, Hirwaun not being at Merthyr, does not directly concern us.

The Williams Locomotive

OUR other snippets of information, however, all seem to refer to Cyfarthfa. On 7 September 1829 William II enquired about entering an engine for the Rainhill trials and on 22 and 29 March 1830 he offered the Liverpool & Manchester a new heavy locomotive.[167] At the same time the opinion was expressed to William II that 'you are all out [i.e. totally astray] in taking up the loco motive Engines'.[168] On 17 July 1830 William Crawshay I complained to his son,

> I fear we are spending too much money in the engineering department. Gurney I see was paid £400 today [for, presumably, the new Hirwaun locomotive]. I tho^t we were equal to all our wants in that way at home and that Will W^{ms} was to have been a racer with one of his own made engines at the Liverpool Race. Sad loss must have accrued by that engine and other such experiments.[169]

William II evidently returned a wounded reply, to which his father responded,

> I did not mean to offend you or direct you beyond your own judgment. I agree it is most necessary to have the means to do our own Engine works. Price's Bills would be most ruinous. We shall therefore continue our establishment for that purpose with respect to loco motive Engines. To buy is like employing Price for fixed Engines. To make one too heavy for our roads was an error in the maker. He knew the strength of the roads and should have made his Engine according. To make engines in Wales to run races in Lancashire is not my wish, or interest, or profession, nor do I think otherwise of having Gurney and his engine into Wales. Pray where do the costs and expences of such things appear?[170]

Price was evidently Joseph Tregelles Price of Neath Abbey, the only south Wales firm outside the ironworks then capable of building engines. But he built none for Cyfarthfa, even stationary ones, between 1820 and 1840.[171] William Williams was a famous Merthyr engineer, 'so obese that he had to be trans-

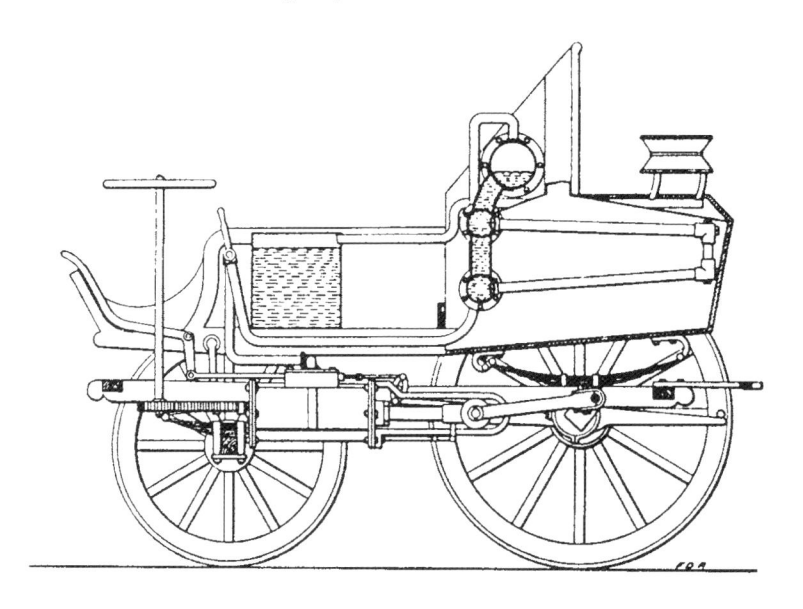

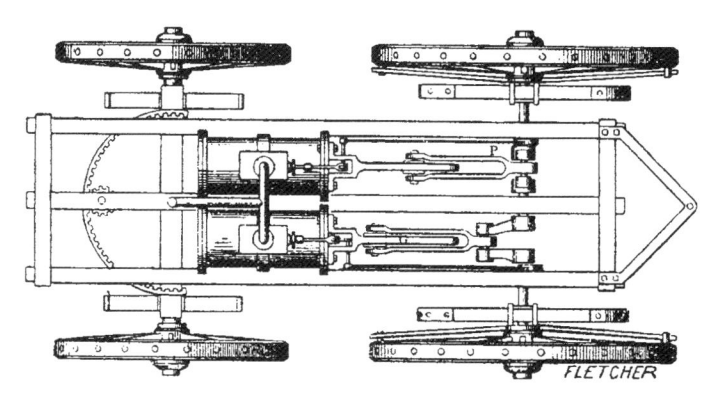

43. Gurney's road drag, 1829.
Elevation: W. Worby Beaumont, *Motor Vehicles and Motors*, 1900, fig.13.
Plan: William Fletcher, *Steam on Common Roads*, 1891, fig.39

ported around the works on a specially constructed trolley'.[172] He was in charge of Cyfarthfa steam engines from at least 1824, and in 1829 completed a pioneer 130-ton hydraulic testing machine there.[173] Not all the Crawshays approved of him. William II's maverick brother George, after a tour of ironworks in Staffordshire in 1832, was reported as commenting snidely that

> We are all prejudiced in Wales. He has seen 50 men as good as old Will Williams, he calls him an old *Fogy*. You can get as good an engineer or mechanic for 50£ a year or anything else better than Will.[174]

Whatever old Will's qualities, it emerges from the sources just quoted that in 1829 he built a locomotive which he and William II considered entering in the Rainhill trials. Next year an engine was offered to the L&M. Also in 1829 or 1830 an over-heavy locomotive broke the rails at Cyfarthfa. How many does this add up to? None of them can be the Gurney machine tested at Hirwaun, which remained Gurney's property and was exceptionally light: a mere 30cwt, two thirds of which was on the driving axle. The phrases 'one of his own made engines' and 'that engine and other such experiments' imply at least two built by Williams before July 1830 at the 'establishment for . . . loco motive Engines'. Moreover, two sizes are implicit. The only plateway gauge known at Cyfarthfa is about 3ft, as shown by wear marks on the present deck of Pontycafnau (FIG.21).[175] The engine which broke the plates, therefore, was probably quite small, whereas the engine (or engines) intended for Rainhill and the L&M must have been built for, or easily convertible to, standard gauge. If it was tested at all it was perhaps at Hirwaun, for Cyfarthfa had neither 4ft 4in. plateways nor the standard gauge, but surely it never worked at either place. Regrettably, no more is heard, or known, of any of these locomotives.

The Gurney Locomotives

Because of the destruction wreaked by his first experiments, one may surmise, William II then turned to Gurney and his light engines, with the trial in March 1830 and the purchase of an engine for Hirwaun in July. But in November he acquired two more slightly heavier ones, at least one of which was constructed by John Braithwaite, the creator (with John Ericsson) of *Novelty* and of the unsuccessful *William IV* and *Queen Adelaide* for the L&M, at his New Road works in London. A possible clue to how Braithwaite and Ericsson came into the equation is found in the L&M board minutes for 17 May 1830: Gurney was negotiating with the railway company about supplying a locomotive and was given 'Heads of Agreement . . . comprising the proposed weight, speed and power nearly similar to the terms of the contract with Captain Ericsson.'[176] Hence, one might speculate, a dialogue between Gurney and Braithwaite and Ericsson that led to their manufacturing his engines, and (as we shall find) to Crawshay's interest in Braithwaite's products.

At all events, on 21 November 1830 William II wrote from Cyfarthfa:

> I have had Mr Gurney's 2 engines here at work about 14 days, and I find every expectation I entertained of the superiority of his boiler is more than realised as far as the production of steam. The engines are drawing, at 3 to 4 miles an hour, 30 to 35 times their own weight [51 to 59½ tons], but whether the rough state of the wheels, or the roads, assists this great superiority at present, we shall better know in another 14 days. However, the engines are quite what I expected and, with 25 tons after them, they have travelled 8 miles an hour, the whole weight of the machine being 34 cwt only, 25 cwt bearing on the working wheels.[177]

On 11 December William II wrote to Gurney requesting the final bill for

> . . . the 2 Engines as my Father & Brothers all wish to know what I am doing. I must of course leave you to determine the Charge you put upon them [between] the Maximum and minimum agreed . . . It appears to me a very great pity that there is no place now, where your Engines can be regularly manufactured for Sale . . . Hoping to hear from you very shortly, that I may settle with you. The Engine at Hirwaun does the work of the 4 Horses in 8 Hours regularly.[178]

The resulting bill came not from Gurney himself but from Braithwaite, with whom on 5 January 1831 William II settled (from his own resources, not the partnership's) the 'account of the little Engine £104 6. 6' and in his covering letter enquired about *William IV*'s performance at Liverpool.[179]

William II, though optimistic in November about his two Gurney locomotives, was soon disillusioned. On 16 March 1831 he wrote of them to Sir Charles Dance, who was operating road coaches between Gloucester and Cheltenham hauled by Gurney drags:

> I am glad to hear you go on as well as you say with the Steamers. Mine are all to pieces and good for nothing until made a new, which I am now about. You will never do any good until the Principle is better carried into effect. I shall claim from the Patentees licence to make 2 Engines in my own way without payment, and I am sure it is all your interest to let me do so. Gurney will never make an engine worth a farthing.[180]

Because the solitary Hirwaun engine was working satisfactorily throughout 1831, these two Gurneys delivered in November 1830 must have been at Cyfarthfa. Indeed, only eleven days before William II wrote to Dance, it was reported that

> A new rail-road, about a mile long, lately made at Cyfarthfa for the purpose of conveying limestone by a locomotive engine from a quarry to the furnaces, is said to be one of the finest roads in the kingdom for the firmness and

44 *(left)*. Gurnos Tramroad: an unusual longitudinal stone sleeper which supported two-and-a-half Outram-style tramplates at a point where the line crossed a small stream (SO 03400818); and **45** *(right)*, a stone sleeper block showing the impression of a smaller and lighter tramplate chair superimposed on the impression of an earlier, larger chair.
Photos: Jonathan Reynolds (2003)

neatness of its construction. The blocks under the rails are about six cwt. each. The road was made according to the instructions and plans of Mr William Williams, the mechanic at Cyfarthfa Works, a man of superior abilities and excellent judgment.[181]

Williams's 'new rail-road' from a limestone quarry a mile away can only be a relaying of the Gurnos line, where archaeology reveals four phases of permanent way: the original edge rails, standard Outram-type cast-iron tramplates (FIG.44), and two stages of wrought-iron plates in lighter and heavier chairs (FIG.45). Outram plates, while still being cast as replacements for existing tramroads, were very out of date by 1831, which seems impossibly late for a whole line to be relaid with them. It is not impossibly early, however, for wrought-iron plates, which were first rolled about 1824[182] and were to become regular on locomotive-worked lines in south Wales.[183] In all likelihood, then, the two Gurney engines acquired in November 1830, and the relaying of the Gurnos Tramroad completed in March 1831, were William II's response to the breakage of plates by the heavy locomotive of which his father had complained the previous summer.

The new or rebuilt Gurney-type locomotives which William II was planning in March 1831, with or without the consent of the patentees, were surely also destined for Gurnos. He was apparently still planning them on 23 February 1832 when he wrote to Dance apropos the design of the Hirwaun Gurney:

> I hope in the course of a few months to apply it to engines and carriages suited to railroads and heavy work so successfully, as to render the advantage of steam-power over that of horses still greater than it is now.[184]

Whether, or in what form, they materialised we cannot be sure, but local memory long recalled a series of early experiments with light locomotives.

> At Cyfarthfa works, for instance, tramways were laid down, and locomotives used, but it was a long time before they could be got into working order. The first were so light that the wheels revolved, and could not be made to go on.[185]

And,

> At Cyfarthfa, for instance, the first engines used would rear up like restive horses instead of keeping to the rails and going ahead. With the next the wheels revolved violently, and that was all. The early ones were more or less defective and ponderous and clumsy, but the idea was right.[186]

The Neath Abbey Locomotive

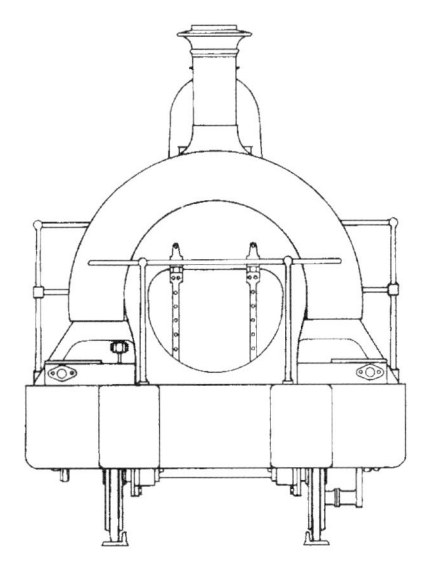

WHATEVER the number and description of these early Cyfarthfa tramroad engines, the tradition long continued. There survives a single Neath Abbey Ironworks drawing for Robert Crawshay of Cyfarthfa, a son of William II, dated 17 July 1871. It shows merely the wheels (2ft 8in. in diameter) and axles for a plateway locomotive with cylinders 8½in. by 16in. and outside eccentrics.[187] The gauge being a little under 3ft between rail flanges, 3ft 1in. over them, and 3ft 2in. between wheel treads, this engine most probably also ran to Gurnos. We may even deduce its appearance. The previous year Neath Abbey had built an 0-4-0 saddle tank for Pascoe Grenfell & Sons of Swansea with cylinders of the same dimensions at identical centres, outside eccentrics, wheels only ¼ inch larger in diameter, and an edge-rail gauge of 3ft 2in. A note on the general arrangement drawing shows that 'future engines' to the same design were anticipated.[188] With no alterations at all, the Swansea engine could be mounted on the Cyfarthfa wheels. It therefore seems highly likely that, wheels and possibly buffers apart, the Cyfarthfa engine was constructed wholly to the Swansea drawings (FIG.46). It was almost the last plateway locomotive to be built anywhere,[189] but otherwise (except perhaps in the Allan straight-link motion and the transverse spring over the rear axle) it was an industrial locomotive utterly typical of its day. Neath Abbey had advanced far from its idiosyncratic designs of the 1830s. Conceivably this engine worked the Gurnos tramroad until Cyfarthfa's closure in 1908, but we do not know.

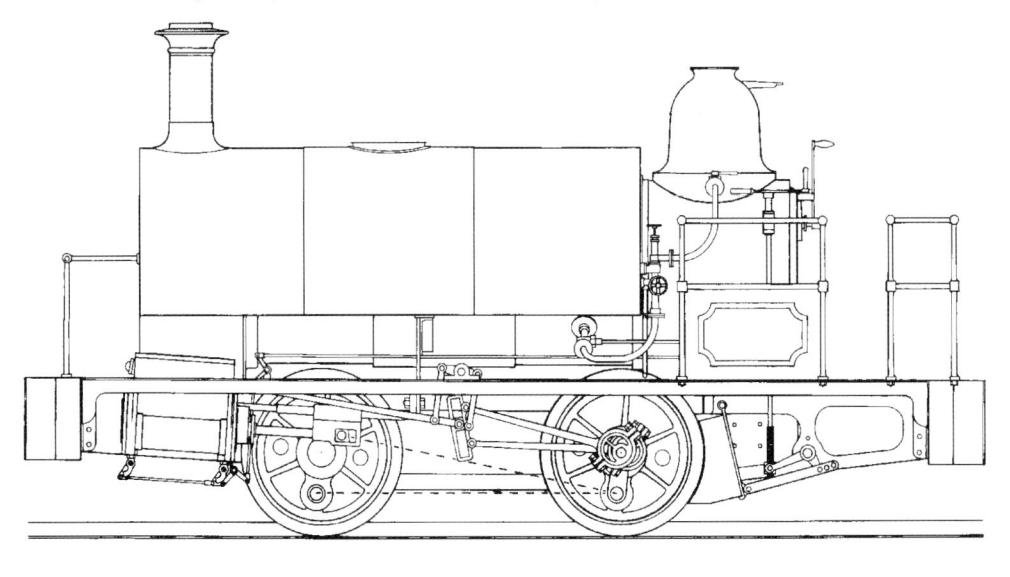

46. Combined drawing of Neath Abbey 0-4-0ST for Pascoe Grenfell and wheels for Cyfarthfa, 1871 (some details not shown).

Dowlais Iron Company Locomotives

Neath Abbey

In 1829, if locomotives were still a rarity, plateway locomotives were even more so. Before that date only about a dozen are known to have existed, of which Trevithick's was the only certain example in Wales. From 1829 onwards, however, while the edge-rail locomotive blossomed mightily, the plateway engine also enjoyed a modest flowering. Thereafter some 70 are known, almost all of which were in south Wales and many of them on the intricate system of tramroads owned by or feeding the Monmouthshire Canal. As a type, they have been sadly neglected, but their builders showed marvellous ingenuity in producing designs suited to the peculiarities of the area, and a major source is available in the large collection of drawings of the Neath Abbey Iron Company. This was a Quaker firm with Cornish connections, founded in 1792, whose works expanded from furnace and foundry to forge and full-blown engineering workshops. Under the guidance of Henry Habberly Price and, as managing partner, his brother Joseph Tregelles Price, it came to supply the industrial market, primarily in south Wales but also further afield, with stationary and marine engines, with iron ships and gas-producing plant, and, in the 50 years from 1830, with at least 50 locomotives both edge and plate.[190] All six of the new engines bought by Dowlais from 1832 to 1838 came from this stable and are consequently quite well documented.[191]

There are many difficulties, however, in using the Neath Abbey drawings. Few at this period are general arrangements, and the vast majority are of components – the pieces, as it were, of a series of jigsaw puzzles. Ideally they bear the names of the customer and locomotive and the date, but many, lacking some or all of these details, are not easy to attribute to the right puzzle. Of some there are conflicting versions, of others the exact location on the locomotive is a matter of deduction, and for some engines many pieces of the puzzle are missing. These drawings, then, are the raw material from which the arrangements presented here have been built up. Historically, too, they are of great interest as perhaps the oldest surviving manufacturing drawings (as distinct from post-production ones) of locomotive components.[192]

Perseverance

The Dowlais letters are incomplete, and are sadly silent over the ordering and development of the first engine. Until it entered service we have to rely on the drawings alone, the first of which is dated 31 August 1831.[193] It seems that the Dowlais engineers gave Neath Abbey a rough specification of the engine they wanted, and that Charles Jordan, the Neath Abbey designer, then translated this into a general design which was returned for criticism to Dowlais who, in this instance, did not accept it.

The drawing in question is (unusually) a general arrangement of an 0-4-4-0 articulated geared rack engine, the rack being for the steep gradients, up to 1 in 16½, on the Dowlais tramroad (FIG.47). The inclined cylinders at the front (20in. stroke and probably 10½in. diameter) drove a central crankshaft, from which gears drove the inner axles of both pivoting bogies, whose wheels were coupled. The drawing shows these gears with straight faces whereas they should be curved. Also on the crankshaft was a small pinion which could be slid either to engage a clutch on the main adhesion gearwheel or to mesh with the rack drive gear, which was carried on a rigid sub-frame. The design – like its successors – thus allowed for either adhesion or rack drive, but not both together. The rack rail lay immediately inside one running rail: not a happy arrangement, for the rack wheel appears to prevent the front bogie from pivoting on a left-hand curve.[194] This is most likely a point overlooked by the designer, who committed an even worse howler in an 1831 design for an Ebbw Vale locomotive in which he put horizontal inside cylinders under the footplate

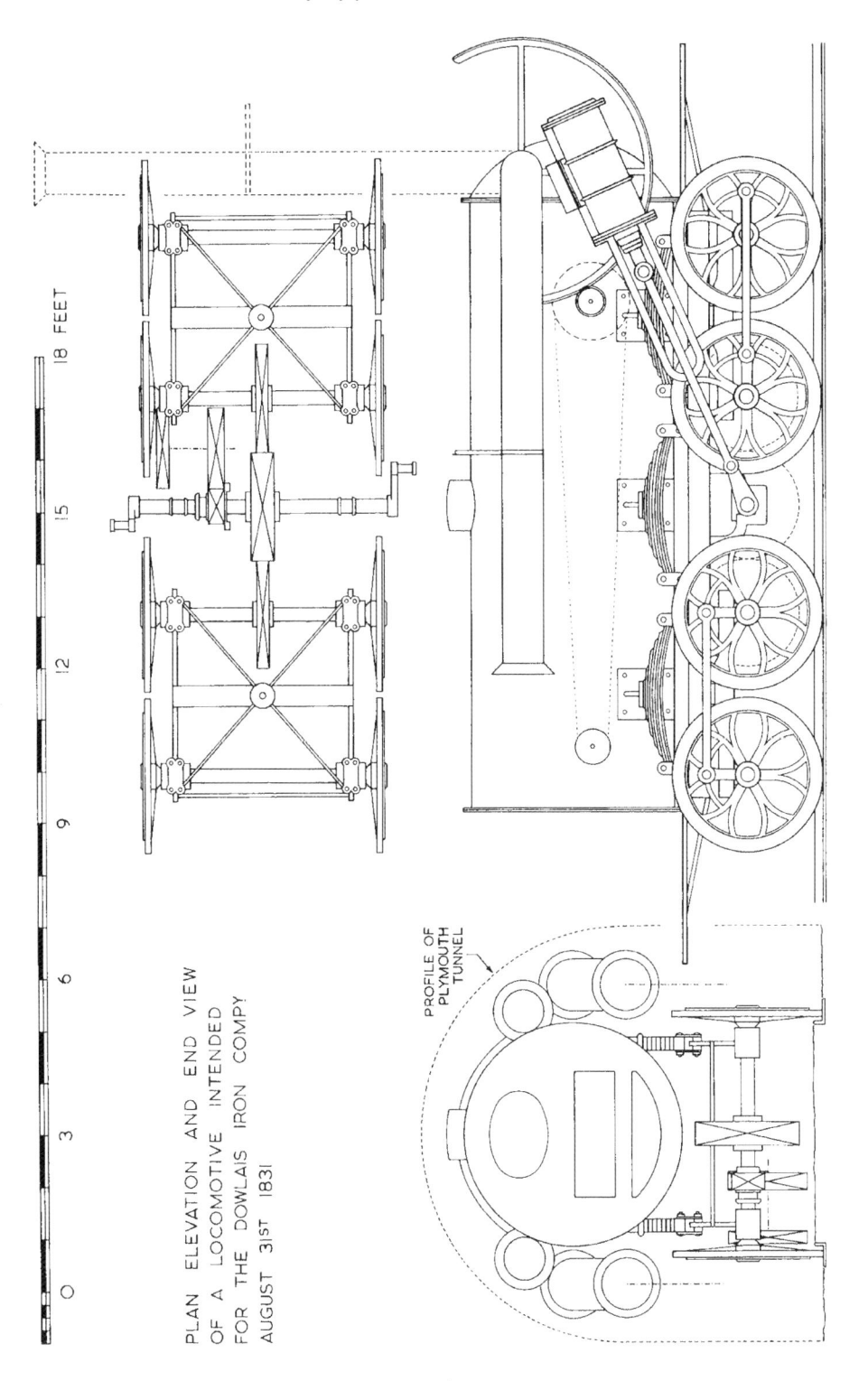

47. Proposed design for Dowlais locomotive, Neath Abbey 1831.

driving forwards to the front axle, oblivious of the fact that the rear axle is in the way.[195]

The springs were set between boiler and main frame, not between wheels and bogie frames. The single-flue boiler had a domed front and a flue-type firebox of typical Neath Abbey pattern. Two chimneys, standing 15ft 7in. above rail level, could be lowered by means of a handle, chain, pinion and toothed semicircle. They were duplicated not to match double flues, as Robert Stephenson had contemplated for *Lancashire Witch*,[196] but to fold down either side of the boiler to fit the Plymouth tunnel, where a single chimney lowered on top of the boiler would still be out of gauge. No details are given of steam pipes or valve gear.

Although the engine was not built in this form, the design was advanced for its day. Rack engines were hitherto restricted to the Blenkinsop and Murray type used on the Middleton and Kenton & Coxlodge waggonways, at Orrell Colliery, perhaps at Nantyglo ironworks, and at two German sites where they failed miserably. Colonel John Stevens had also built an experimental rack engine in America. All these were rack only, with no adhesion drive. It was Neath Abbey which introduced the idea of using rack as an auxiliary drive for steep gradients. The concept of the bogie was developed and (in 1812) patented by William Chapman. Before 1831 it was certainly applied to his Heaton locomotive and arguably to his Lambton and Whitehaven ones and to the famous eight-wheeled Wylam engines. These perhaps apart, this was also the first time an articulated locomotive was envisaged, though the first to be built was Horatio Allen's *South Carolina* of 1832. Although rejected by Dowlais, the design was revived by Neath Abbey in a locomotive built for the Rhymney Iron Company in 1838, with a similar basic arrangement but rear cylinders, fixed chimney and no rack.[197]

Dowlais was quick in turning down the plan, for on 14 September 1831 Neath Abbey produced another drawing for a rather simpler engine. It approaches the final design as actually built in the form of *Perseverance*, to be described shortly; but it has a shorter boiler, a shorter wheelbase and a flat front to the boiler with a small and awkward smokebox near the base from which a vertical flue rises to a pair of swivelling chimneys. Evidently this design met with approval from the Dowlais engineer, who endorsed the drawing for the guidance of Neath Abbey:

The Engine including boiler wheels &c complete not to exceed 8 Tons. The difference in level of the Boiler in some parts of the Road will be 2 Ins p Yard [1 in 18]. The Horizontal Tubes would be preferred in the Boiler if Mess. Neath Abbey Co who are responsible for the performance of the Engine think proper. Speed of Engine 7 Miles p hour. The Engine to be rec[eive]d to put on the Road before the 25th March.[198]

Having established the general idea, Neath Abbey proceeded to amend the design in most of its details, and there are no more general arrangements. Instead, there is a series of 50 drawings of components dated (where they bear a date at all) between 14 October 1831 and 23 May 1832. They leave uncertain the precise location of the dome, steam manifold and feed pump, and for some parts, notably the safety valve, control levers and chimney winch, there are no drawings at all.[199]

The original name given to this engine was *Success*, but in May 1832, before it was finished, the name was changed. On several drawings 'Success' has been crossed out and such words added as 'now called Perseverance'. In the very same month several drawings of *Industry*, then being built for Harford Davies & Co. of Ebbw Vale, were altered in precisely the same way. Both engines were 0-6-0s with 10½in. cylinders, lowering chimneys, and the same gauge; and it is quite possible that only one of them should have had its name changed. Which? 'Perseverance' was the motto not only of the Sirhowy Tramroad, in which the Harfords had a large stake, but also of the Glamorganshire Canal Company, with which the Merthyr Tramroad was in rivalry. Whatever the truth, the name *Perseverance* stuck to the Dowlais engine; whether it did to the Ebbw Vale one is not certain.

The Dowlais *Perseverance* (FIG.48) was a geared 0-6-0, with cast-iron wheels 3ft 1in. in diameter of the 'gothic' pattern favoured by Neath Abbey. Its frame, like most of its successors', was singularly slight, made of flat bar iron 3in. by 1in. with stayed cross members near the ends to which the coupling bars were attached. The boiler had plates ⅜in. thick and a slightly domed front (as did *Speedwell* of 1830 on the Sirhowy and indeed earlier Stephenson engines).[200] There were probably water tubes across a single large flue, a design perhaps initiated by Hackworth in his *Globe* for the Stockton & Darlington in 1830.[201] It seems that Neath Abbey offered the choice between

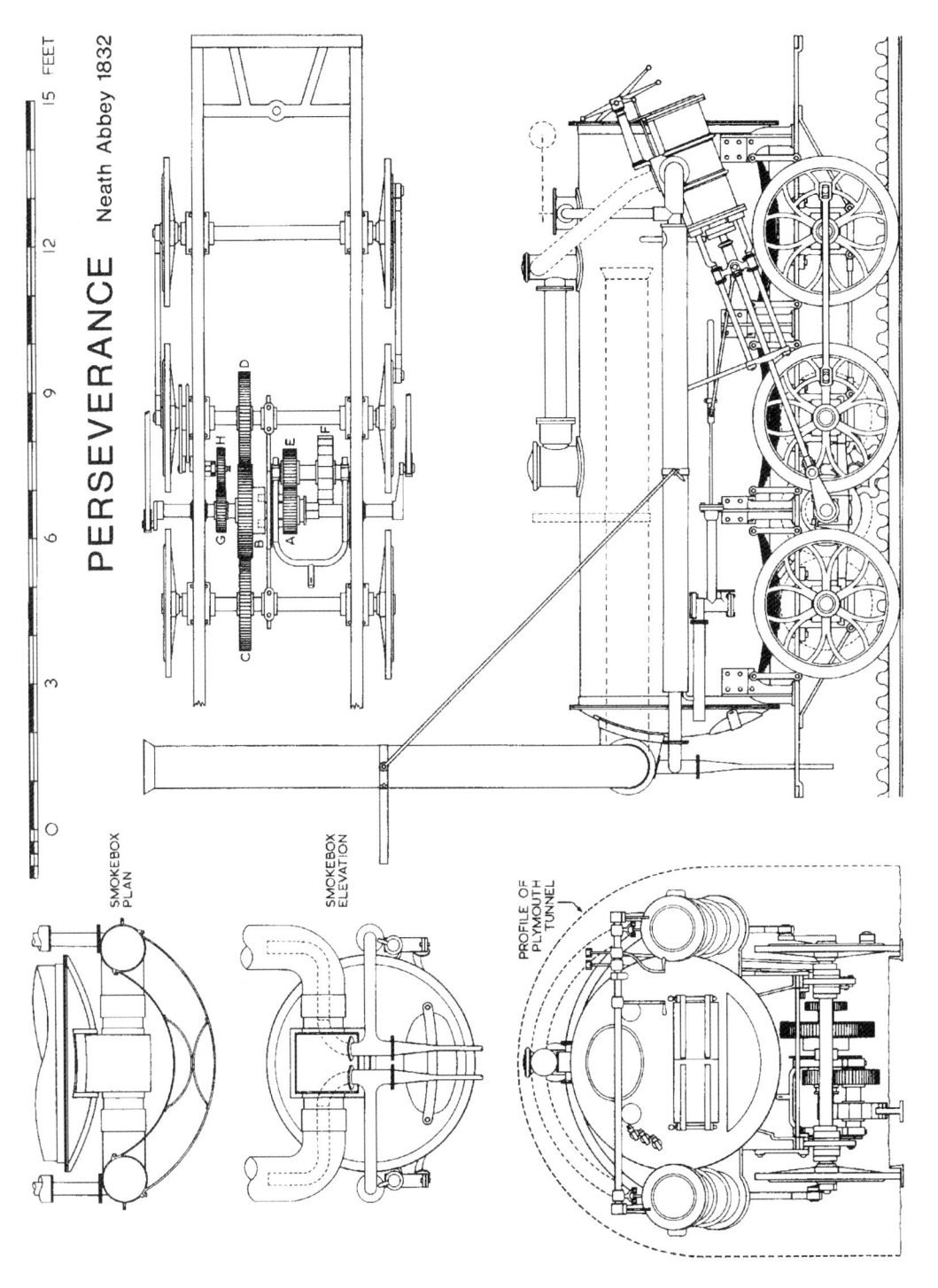

Merthyr Tydfil Tramroads and their Locomotives

48. *Perseverance, Neath Abbey 1832*

vertical and horizontal water tubes. Dowlais, as we have seen, expressed a preference for 'Horizontal Tubes' (and in 1834 was supplied with spare 'tubes' for *Perseverance*),[202] whereas for the contemporary *Royal William* the proprietors of the Gloucester & Cheltenham Tramroad opted for the vertical.[203] The working pressure is not recorded for any Dowlais engine, but on the Neath Abbey locomotives for the Bodmin & Wadebridge it was 50psi.[204]

In a departure from Neath Abbey's early preference for vertical cylinders and a bell-crank drive, or horizontal cylinders and a rocking beam drive, the cylinders (10½in. by 20in.) were inclined and set at the back of the boiler, a position copied directly, perhaps, from *Britannia* at Tredegar and the Penydarren Company's locomotive. The crankshaft was mounted on bearing frames attached at either end to the horn blocks of the front two axles, so that it was sprung. It carried the driving pinion A, which could be slid sideways along a square section of the shaft by a sheave operated by crank and rod from the footplate. For adhesion drive, pinion A engaged gear B (which was loose on the crankshaft) by means of a clutch, and B drove the front two axles by gears C and D, while the rear axle was driven by coupling rods. For rack drive, B was left idling and A was slid back to mesh with gear E on a short axle which carried the rack wheel F. When not in use, the rack axle was raised to clear pointwork. Its bearings were mounted on a U-frame, whose opposite end was raised or lowered by lever from the footplate. The U-frame was carried centrally on two large hoops, one attached to a crankshaft bearing frame, the other to a similar sub-frame between the main axles; the latter hoop was wide enough to allow pinion A to slide through it. By adhesion, *Perseverance* travelled 9ft 8in. per revolution of the crank, by rack 3ft 11in. The cast-iron rack rail, with teeth at 6in. pitch, was laid with its centre line 14in. from the outer face of the running rail.

The details of the valve motion are not precisely given, but they seem to have followed contemporary Neath Abbey practice in those days before link motion or even gabs. Pinion G on the crankshaft drove gear H. The axle of gear H was mounted on a bracket attached to the crankshaft bearing frame (and was thus sprung) and had two small-throw cranks at the end, from which rods transmitted the motion to the 'Y-shafts' mounted on top of the boiler backplate. From here rocker arms actuated the slide valves. There was no variable cut-off. Gear H was loose on the valve crankshaft, which was hollow. Inside it was a sliding spindle with lugs projecting through slots in the shaft. These lugs, when the spindle was pushed in, engaged in key-ways in the boss of H which in turn rotated the shaft. When the spindle was pulled out (via a crank, a rod, and probably a treadle on the footplate), the lugs coincided with a hollow ring in the boss and H turned freely without driving the shaft. To reverse, the driver put H out of drive, worked the valve cranks through 180° by means of handles on the Y-shaft, and put H back into drive. To stop, since the engine had no brakes, he put H out of drive, waited for half a revolution of the main crank, and put it back into drive. In both cases the valve sequence was reversed. Braking by means of reversing the engine, common practice with early locomotives, must have imposed a considerable strain on the working gear, but speeds were low.

We do not know the precise arrangement of the controls for operating the drive clutch, rack lowering arm, or reversing gear. The whole design, though compact and ingenious, was made awkward by being sprung. In *Dowlais*, the next rack engine, though a similar set-up was retained, the gearing was not sprung. *Perseverance*'s hollow-shaft reversing clutch was particularly curious, and it is no surprise that it was replaced by a more conventional clutch in 1840.

The boiler front carried a box which held the swivels of the two chimneys. These reached a height of about 16ft above the rails, were held up by diagonal stays, and (according to the invoice) were raised by winch, though the drawings give no comprehensible details. The safety valve, which vented into the exhaust pipe and surely made the engine steam even harder when it blew off, was apparently of standard Neath Abbey dead-weight type, utterly susceptible to the locomotive's motion – and plateway engines on yard-long rails must have bounced maniacally. The boiler feed pump, actuated by a small rod off the cross-head, pushed water drawn from the tender through water heaters surrounding the exhaust pipes. The two exhaust pipes passed into the chimney support box and were bent up in short swivelling blast pipes, each in its own chimney; these pipes were parallel, not nozzled. Since the feed-water heaters would cause some condensation of exhaust steam, each exhaust pipe had a downward-pointing pipe at the boiler front through which the condensate could run off. These pipes being much longer than the blast pipes and finely nozzled, there would be little loss of blast.

The engine had a 'casing', probably wooden-strip boiler lagging.[205] Of the tender, nothing is known except that it was four-wheeled, and on each axle one wheel was fixed and one loose. But no doubt it resembled those of later Dowlais engines, for Neath Abbey tenders were of standard design. Those on the Bodmin & Wadebridge held 370 gallons of water and a ton of coal and weighed 5½ tons full.[206]

Perseverance was evidently delivered, in a dismantled state, early in June 1832, by sea from Neath to Cardiff and perhaps by canal from there. The detailed invoice, dated 5 June, reads:[207]

A Locomotive Engine with 2 10½" Cylinders fitted with metallic spring pistons, Tank for Water, fitted with copper and leather pipes, cocks, Hitcher and casing as p agreemt	£630
Machinery for ascending Dowlais Hill, consisting of Tooth wheels, pinions, bored and faced, axles turned with cranks bored and wrought iron carriages of best faggoted iron, many parts being bored turned and faced for concentric motion, fitted with brasses, bored holes for do, double nutted and fitted with stops including patterns for wheels, levers, spindles and carr[ia]g[e]s for disengaging pinions, Engineers time designing &c	£75
Extra for 2 stacks to lower, much additional labour, copper pipes, joints turned and bored, stays, levers for lifting with winch complete	£10
Tender on springs, Wheels with casehardened Naves and Rims, axles turned and fitted with steel washers, tool box with Hinges and lock	£40
2 screwjacks with screws of best thread turned and cut in lathe, wood boxes iron hooped and spanner complete	£5.5.0
7 spanners for engine of various sizes 2q 3lb @ 5d	£1.4.7
12 spare screws 2/- 2 chisels 1 point 1 drill 7/-	9.0
1 Hammer steel'd 2/6 Drill Brace and Dog 3/6 ½in. tap 4/-	10.0
	£762.8.7

For assembling and testing the engine at Dowlais there was in addition £12 15s 0d for two fitters' time, plus Charles Jordan's time and expenses which Dowlais paid him direct. Under pressure, Neath Abbey deducted the £10 extra for the swivelling stacks. Dowlais paid £760 in July, and Neath Abbey generously forewent the remaining £5 3s 7d.[208]

By the end of July *Perseverance* was ready to show its paces. The *Hereford Times* for 4 August 1832 recorded that

> The Dowlais Iron Company's steam carriage 'Powerful' lately left the Dowlais works for the bason, a distance of eleven miles, with one hundred and twenty-six tons of iron attached to it, exclusive of engine, tender, and trams, together more than two hundred tons; the Powerful returned with forty-seven empty trams, and performed the journey to and fro, within twelve hours. – This engine is considered to be the most powerful of any in the country. The very skilful engineer Mr. Gardner, anticipates his being able to perform the journey with two hundred tons of iron, exclusive of carriages; should he accomplish this, the performance will be unprecedented in the history of locomotives.

There being no other evidence for an engine named *Powerful* and this account being so similar to the next, it seems that the reporter simply got the name wrong. *The Cambrian* on 18 August, reminding readers that the Penydarren Company's *Eclipse* had on 22 June hauled 23 tons down the tramroad, reported:

> We are now credibly informed, that the *Eclipse* is *eclipsed* by the *Perseverance*, got up by the Neath Abbey Iron Co., and supplied with the assistance of a Rack running parallel with the tram plates from Pennydarren to the Dowlais Works. This engine has accomplished the amazing task of conveying from the Dowlais Works to the basin aforesaid, 126 tons of iron, besides the weight of the engine, tender and waggons 50¾ tons, making an aggregate of 177 tons. The engine, after waiting several hours for the discharge of iron, returned to the works with her complement of empty waggons, and ascended the side of the mountain, by means of the Rack, with ease, without stopping for steam. The fact is the more remarkable from the road winding in some places excessively, so that the engine might be seen to have passed in one place two reverse arcs, one of 30½, the other 40 yards radius, at a distance of 146 yards a head of the last loaded waggon in the train; and from the first nine miles

of the road from the basin having an ascent of from 1¾ to 7¼in. in a chain [1 in 453 to 1 in 109], and the last two miles 25½ to 48⅛ inches per chain [1 in 31 to 1 in 16½], up this last part the engine works at its usual speed, but drawing its load at 2–5ths of the speed it makes on the other parts of the way. It is supposed that the *Perseverance* will take down 200 tons at a time, and convey her empty trams back to the Works, when a sufficient number of carriages with springs are prepared. It is well known that the Welsh mountains supply an immence store of the *corn* these *iron horses* require to sustain them, and having so barren a surface, it is only astonishing that the natives, or some of their more knowing tenantry, did not discover before this period the possibility of sending their mineral produce to the margin of the sea for shipment by less tedious means than canals, and locks, and apply the waters that flow down the valley, in performing mechanical operations, for which they appear by nature so admirably adapted.

Perseverance's magnificent train must have included about 60 trams. Given that it was pulling its load downhill, its performance might be thought unremarkable. But it must be remembered that it was on an old and worn plateway, where the frictional resistance might approach three times that on cast-iron edge rails.²⁰⁹ A contemporary account of a journey behind this, the first combined adhesion/rack locomotive, will be found in the final section.

In 1840–1, as the drawings show, the engine was given a considerable rebuild, with alterations to the rack and reversing gear, a heavier frame, a single chimney folding forwards, and a new set of coupling bars attached to a central cross member on the frame. But it bore the same general appearance to the end of its days.

Yn Barod Etto

No sooner had *Perseverance* arrived than Dowlais was in search of a smaller, simpler engine. On 11 August 1832 a tender was submitted by R. Jones of Birmingham (late of Nantyglo, who was currently building a locomotive for the Baileys' limestone tramroad from Llangattock):

> I will supply you with a Locomotive Engine to the weight you want, working upon 4 wheels & Springs with Metalick pistons and fitted up in a superior style of Workmanship, deliver'd at Bristol and put to work for the sum of 350 pounds. I would advise you to have one 4½ tons, including the water in Boiler and the cistern to carry water to suply the Boiler. I am now making one for Mr Bailey of Nanty Glo to the above weight, if your road will bear that weight it will be preferable to the other, the price will be the same. I will warrant it to keep a sufficient supply of Steam and draw as much as any Engine in the Kingdom of its weight on the same road.²¹⁰

Dowlais endorsed his letter 'Too high a price'. On the same day Robert Stephenson & Co. wrote:

> One of your agents called here a short time ago & requested us to send you our prices for Locomotive Engines, to suit the Rail Roads of which our Engineer, who was at Penydarran [in connection with *Eclipse*], brought the dimensions. As our Mr R. Stephenson is expected here in a week or so, and there are some points on which we would like to consult him, we think it best to defer sending an Estimate till he returns.²¹¹

Both Jones and Stephenson were too late, for on 27 July Neath Abbey had confirmed an order which Dowlais had just placed for

> ... a Locomotive Engine of 2 – 8½" Cylinders to run on 4 wheels adapted for a Rail as well as Tram Road – to be ready on the 23rd of October subject to a fine of 5£ p week for all time after that period. The price for the same to be £420 – we confirm the arrangement made by C. Jordan but the delivery must be on board *here*. We proceed with it at once.²¹²

Named *Yn Barod Etto* ('Ever-ready') it was a straightforward affair compared to *Perseverance*. It was not geared, the rear cylinders, 8½in. by 20in., driving direct to the front axle. The four-coupled wheels, designed to run on either plate or edge rail as explained in FIG.50, were 2ft 10in. in diameter on the edge wheel tread and 3ft 4in. over the flanges. Since there was no rack, and there are no signs that the chimney could be lowered, *Yn Barod Etto* was no doubt destined for the 4ft 4in. tramroads around Dowlais works and for the intended standard-gauge railway from Morlais quarry.

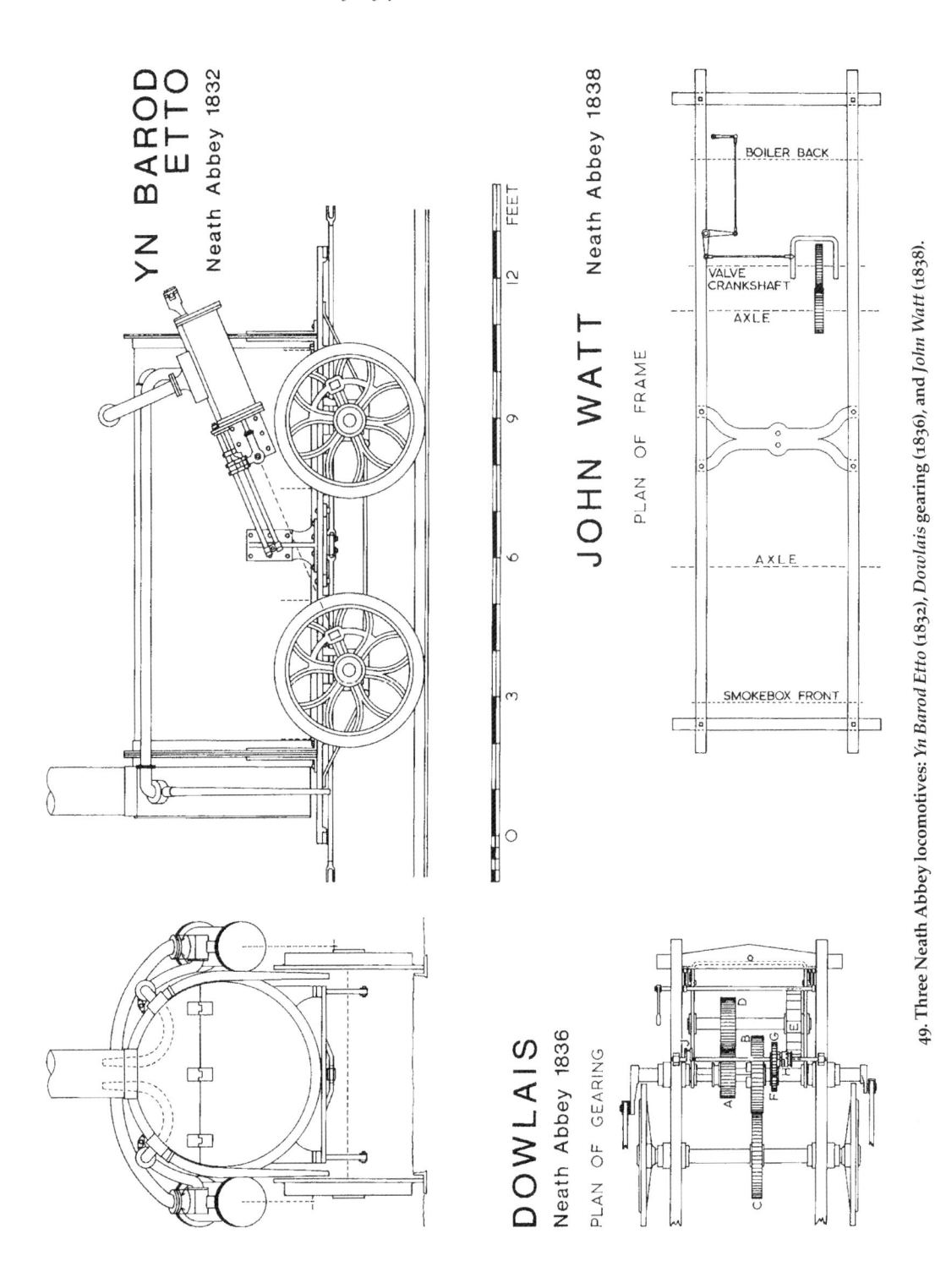

49. Three Neath Abbey locomotives: *Yn Barod Etto* (1832), *Dowlais* gearing (1836), and *John Watt* (1838).

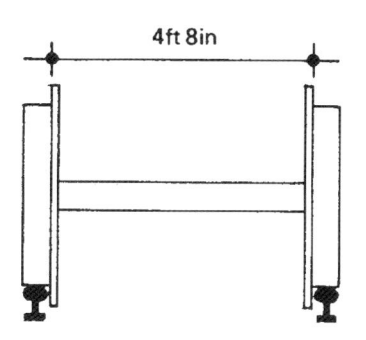

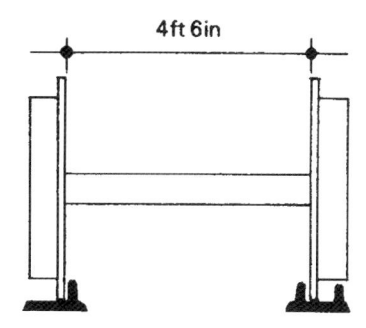

50. Combined edge/plate wheels (diagrammatic only).
When running on plate rails, if the wheel flanges were of the normal depth (1 inch or thereabouts), the broad treads would foul the flanges of the rails and check rails at points. The wheel flanges were therefore made exceptionally deep (3 inches) to raise the treads clear.

Because only ten drawings survive (all of separate parts, dated between 1 August and 4 October 1832) the overall picture of this engine is far from complete (FIG.49). The frames, $1^3/_8$in. thick, were a little heavier than *Perseverance*'s, and a central cross member held the coupling bars. The boiler, with a proper smokebox, was almost certainly multitubular. The twin blast pipes were slightly nozzled. The Y-shaft, no doubt driven by pinion and crank again, was mounted on the cylinder ends. There were probably feed-water heaters round the exhaust pipes, but we have no information about the boiler mountings or the tender. The name was painted on a board on each side. The engine and 'tank' – presumably tender – were shipped from Neath to Cardiff at a freight of £10 on 8 November 1832 (two weeks late), and again Charles Jordan was sent to superintend the trials, other workmen being afraid to go to Dowlais because of the cholera raging there.[213]

Mountaineer

In December 1832 Charles Jordan was already angling for another order[214] but, if he got it then, there was a delay, for the eleven drawings of components are dated from 9 July to 17 September 1833. *Mountaineer* (FIG.51) was generally similar to *Yn Barod Etto* but an 0-6-0. Because the chimney was hinged and the drawings include a profile of the tunnel, *Mountaineer* was intended for use on the Merthyr Tramroad, though it had no rack for the Dowlais Tramroad. The frames were a reversion to the *Perseverance* size of 3in. by 1in. The wheels were 3ft 4in. and, though the drawings show no details, they must have been for plate rails only, for they were set too close together to leave room for flanges. The boiler was closely similar to that of *Charles Jordan* (FIG.53) but had 33 parallel tubes (replacement tubes were pressed to 120psi).[215] The horse power was $8^1/_2$; the cylinders were $8^1/_2$in. by 20in.; there were apparently feed-water heaters (although there are no drawings of pipe-work); and the single chimney folded forwards and was held up by a stay probably fixed to the dome. There is a complete drawing of the tender, of standard Neath Abbey design with a tank on top and, unlike the locomotive, dual-purpose wheels with an edge gauge of 4ft $8^1/_2$in.

Mountaineer cost £450 (probably excluding the tender) and was sent in February 1834 by sea to Cardiff, where it (or part of it) met with the misfortune of being dropped into the ship's hold during unloading. Neath Abbey had to supply two new wheels and other items to repair the damage – small objects like these were sent by cart to Pont Walby at the head of the Neath valley, where a Dowlais cart picked them up. On 8 March 1834 Charles Jordan junior went to Dowlais 'for putting the Mountaineer Engine in order and when complete his father will be up to start her'.[216]

Dowlais's next locomotive, being a purely standard-gauge one, is of only marginal interest to us. In 1835 the Liverpool & Manchester's *Etna*, a *Planet*-type 2-2-0 with 5ft wheels built by Stephensons in 1830, was sold second-hand to Guest Lewis & Co.[217] It was intended, presumably, for the standard-gauge railways to Morlais quarry and around the works, although the price of £250 seems extraordinarily high for a locomotive quite inappropriate for the purpose.

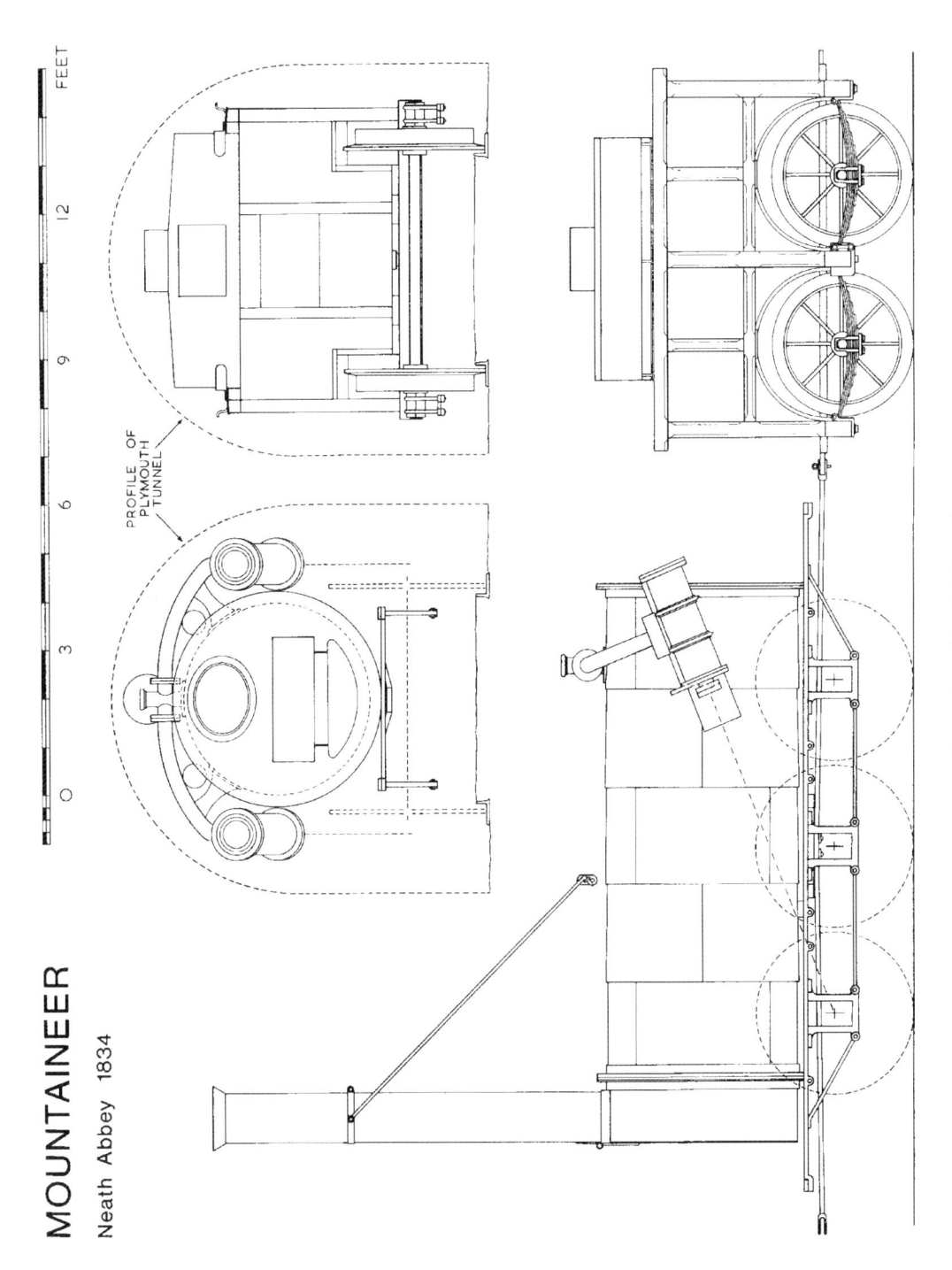

Merthyr Tydfil Tramroads and their Locomotives

MOUNTAINEER
Neath Abbey 1834

FEET

PROFILE OF PLYMOUTH TUNNEL

51. *Mountaineer*, Neath Abbey 1834.

Dowlais

A year after the delivery of *Mountaineer*, another rack engine was contemplated. Neath Abbey wrote to Dowlais on 19 January 1835:

> Our price for a Locomotive Engine of the same power as the 'Mountaineer' will be £500 – we had 450£ for that but lost nearly 50£ by it and we could not make another for less than £500 – delivery and payment as before. We cannot say the cost of the machinery requisite for working on the Rack as it is a point that requires a good deal of consideration and had best be decided on by your as well as our Engineer – when the mode of doing it is fixed we will give you an estimate.[218]

The design for the rack gearing was hammered out in February, but for some reason a long delay ensued.[219] On 29 September Neath Abbey responded to Dowlais's impatience:

> We have 10 or 12 good workmen on your Locomotive Engine – almost every part is cast and bored or forged – The fitting it together is of course more tedious and it is almost impossible to say to a week how long it will take, but we hope to have the steam up in 6 or 7 weeks – sooner if possible.[220]

It was not finished until January 1836, and even then Dowlais quibbled about the bill for the rack gear, claiming that it was the design of their own engineer and that Neath Abbey's charge was excessive. This broke down to £3 3s 6d for materials and labour, £24 17s 3d for fitting (almost 100 man-days at 5s), and £6 6s 0d for Charles Jordan's time in making drawings (12 days at 10s 6d). But the bill – a total of £604 19s 1d probably including the tender – was paid, under protest.[221]

The engine was named *Dowlais* (sometimes referred to as No.4). There survive 28 drawings of components, dated between 20 June and 23 December 1835; but

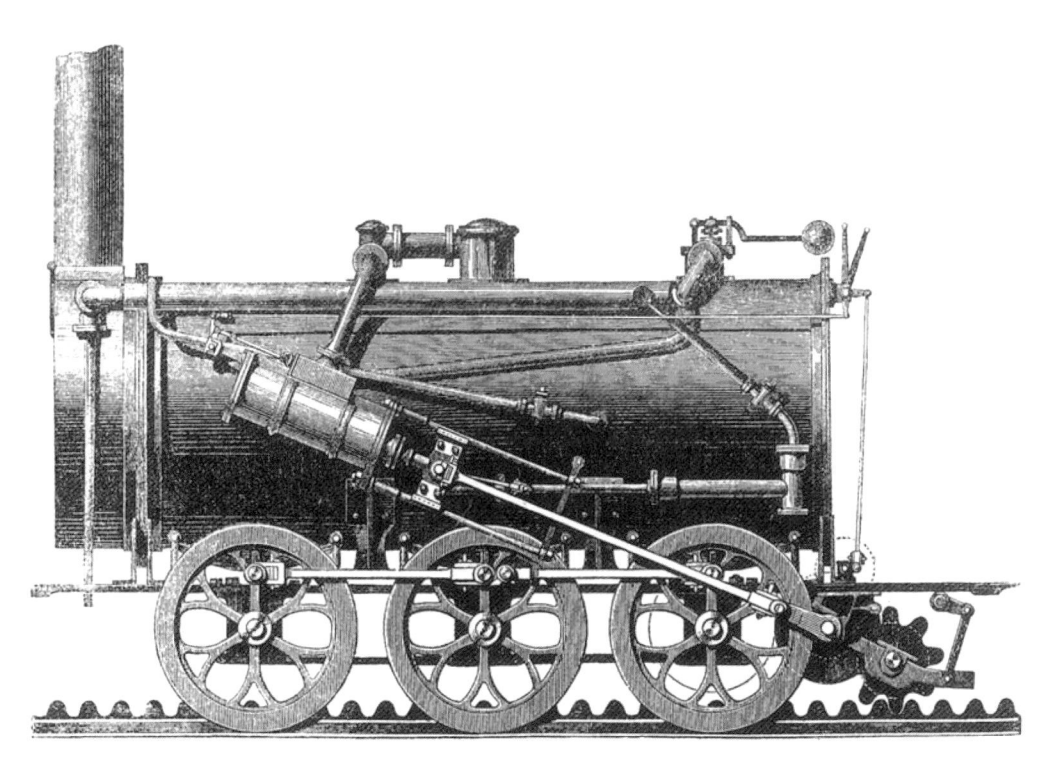

52. *Dowlais*, Neath Abbey 1836.
From: *Engineering*, 15 November 1867, p.457

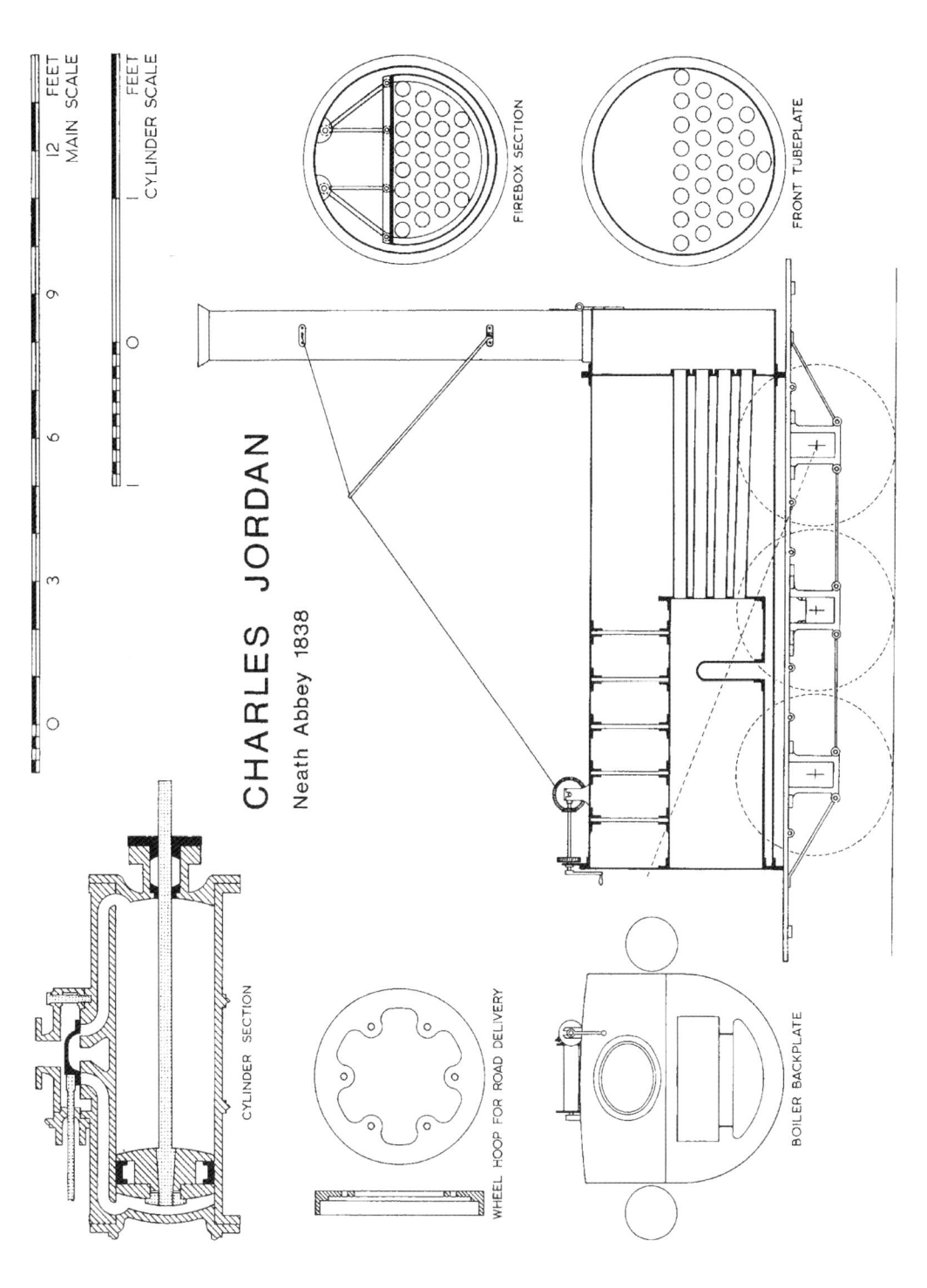

Merthyr Tydfil Tramroads and their Locomotives

53. *Charles Jordan*, Neath Abbey 1838.

thirty years later an almost complete side elevation was published in *Engineering* (FIG.52).²²² This omits most of the controls and a few details like the coupling bars and the diagonal support stays from the boiler back to the footplate. In much of its design *Dowlais* resembled its predecessors – the front view of the smokebox, for example, was identical to that of *Yn Barod Etto* – and the force pump and feed-water heaters followed the usual pattern. The six-coupled wheels, for plate rail only, were 3ft 1in., the framing was 3in. by 1³/₈in., the boiler was almost identical to *Mountaineer*'s with 33 tubes but 5in. longer, and the cylinders – at the front for a change – were 8½in. by 18in. The single chimney could be lowered forwards by a roller and chain winch with a ratchet, though this is mentioned only in a letter, not in the drawings. The tender was virtually identical to *Mountaineer*'s, with edge/plate wheels.

Dowlais is most interesting, however, for the very compact rack mechanism, which is more clearly seen in the plan (FIG.50) than in the *Engineering* engraving. On the crankshaft was a pinion A which could be slid along a key-way by means of a crank and a handle that was held in a three-notched quadrant in neutral, rack or adhesion. For adhesion drive the spokes of A were engaged in the clutch of the pinion B, which was loose on the crankshaft and permanently meshed with the gear C fixed on the rear axle. When driving the rack, pinion A meshed with gear D on the rack spindle, the rack wheel E being 1ft 3½in. in pitch diameter. The rack spindle was mounted on a U-frame held at the front by bearings on the crankshaft and raised or lowered by crank and rods actuated by a 4ft lever on the footplate. The third gear on the crankshaft, F, was fixed. It was always in mesh with the gear G that was loose on the valve working shaft; G could be engaged at diametrically opposite positions by the sliding clutch H, which was held open against a spring by a pedal on the footplate. Two cranks of 2⅛in. throw transmitted the drive from the working shaft to the Y-shaft with its handles, and rockers from there operated the valves. The driver reversed and braked in the same way as on *Perseverance*. *Dowlais* moved 8ft 9in. per revolution of the crankshaft by adhesion, or 3ft 7in. by rack. By May 1837 new gear wheels were already required.²²³

After the debacle with *Mountaineer* at Cardiff, Neath Abbey dispatched *Dowlais* on 19 January 1836 by road. William Baker, the haulier employed, was understandably fearful about conveying so large a chunk of ironmongery, and demanded £21 for the job plus expenses plus keep for his horses. The distance involved – up the Vale of Neath and over the upland road between the valleys which reached a height of 1,178ft – was 24 miles. Dowlais in turn was dubious about the cost, but Neath Abbey pointed out that the freight by sea would be at least £30 and that it might be a month before they could get the services of either of the two ships they knew of which could accommodate a locomotive. Neath Abbey sent four men to accompany the engine. *Dowlais* was hauled along the road on its own wheels, to which were bolted specially-cast hoops with treads 6in. wide to avoid rutting the surface. Presumably the journey was completed without undue disaster, for on 19 March 'the Tender for your 'Dowlais' Locomotive Engine is sent up by Wm Baker this day – its weight is 2 Tons and we could not get him to take it for less than 1/9 p ton p mile.'²²⁴

Charles Jordan

THE next engine, No.5, was called after the Neath Abbey engineer and boasted cast nameplates. There are 15 drawings dated from 14 August 1837 to 13 February 1838. Much like *Mountaineer*, it was a straightforward 0-6-0 without a rack (FIG.53). Although no details survive, the 3ft 4½in. wheels were for plate rail only; the framing was again 3in. by 1in., and the coupling bars started at a central cross-member. Unlike *Mountaineer*'s, the boiler had only 26 tubes which, in a surprisingly sophisticated manner for so early a date, splayed out towards the front tubeplate. The long semicircular flue-type firebox had a large grate area and a midfeather forming a small combustion chamber – almost a predecessor of the firebrick arch?²²⁵

The boiler backplate was not circular, but extended upwards to a rectangular top for the easier support of the Y-shaft. Details of the valve motion are entirely lacking, but a section of the 8½in. by 20in. cylinder shows that the slide valve had only a nominal steam lap (⅛in., with ports 1 inch long and a valve travel of 2¼in.) and no exhaust lap. There was apparently no lead. Expansive working was therefore minimal, which need not surprise us as the function of valve lap was in those days hardly understood. The piston rings, as in the earlier engines, were of brass and in three parts, tightened by triangular wedges after the method adopted by George (or Isaac?) Dodds in 1831. The chimney folded forwards and was raised and lowered by a chain wound on a roller at the boiler back, which the driver turned by a crank handle and bevel gears, and a stay gave the necessary angle to lift the chimney from the horizontal – the sketch is delightfully annotated 'the Stak to bee lourd for goyn throo the tunnell'. The tender was doubtless of the standard design.

Like *Dowlais*, *Charles Jordan* was delivered by road. On 16 February 1838 a document was signed:

> It is agreed between William Baker & the Neath Abbey Iron Company on behalf of Guest Lewis & Company that the latter shall pay the former for taking a 6 Wheeled Locomotive Engine to Dowlais, the same price as he received for the 'Mountaineer' Engine about 4 years ago, & that he shall be paid £4.10 for the Tender. The Dowlais Company to send 4 men to accompany the Engine. W. Baker to bring back any Tools or Apparatus taken from Neath Abbey.[226]

The mention of *Mountaineer*, which travelled by sea, must be a mistake for *Dowlais* only two years before. Hoops – of a different design from those for *Dowlais* – were again attached to the wheels for the journey, but the drawing of them is mysterious, since their outer diameter makes them too large for the close-set wheels. It could have been managed by removing the centre wheels, but six hoops were cast. The springs seem to have suffered in the process, as a month later Dowlais was ordering replacements for *Charles Jordan*.[227]

John Watt

THE last Dowlais engine from Neath Abbey was No.6, *John Watt*, named after the Dowlais engineer who seems have been responsible for transport matters from this time. There are eleven drawings of parts, ranging in date from 22 November 1837 to 9 April 1838, which leave major gaps in our knowledge (FIG.50). The engine was something of a cross between *Yn Barod Etto* and *Charles Jordan*, with four wheels like the former but a long boiler identical to the latter's. This resulted in large overhangs: 4ft in front of and 5ft 2in. behind the 5ft 6in. wheelbase. The framing, 3in. by 2½in., was much heavier than on its predecessors. The cylinder diameter was 8½in., the stroke uncertain but probably the usual 20in. The drive was to the front wheels, and from the rear axle a pair of gears drove the valve working shaft. The driven gear was engaged by one of two clutches on either side of it, which were moved sideways by a bow frame worked by levers from the footplate. Connecting rods from cranks on the working shaft ran up beside the boiler in the usual way to oscillate the Y-shaft, which was a copy of that on *Dowlais*. There was no rack. The tender, with edge/plate wheels, was almost identical to *Mountaineer*'s and, like *Yn Barod Etto*, *John Watt* seems to have operated in and around the works.

It was tested in steam at Neath Abbey on 11 April 1838 and, on 24 April, the makers wrote:

> Your Locomotive Engine is cased [lagged] and is now being painted. Chas Jordan is of opinion that he can attach pieces of wood to the springs so as to render its going up the road quite safe [apparently referring back to the trouble with *Charles Jordan*'s springs] . . . C. Jordan thinks it must go up to your works as it will not fit the tramroad from the village [Penydarren].

William Baker again did the transport (£23 for the engine, £4 for the tender) and left for Dowlais on 2 May 1838. But there was trouble with *John Watt*'s gauge. On 10 May Neath Abbey wrote:

> Our Engineer Chas Jordan informs us that he had intended to put the last locomotive Engine Wheels to 4f 8 guage and indeed they were actually fixed so and afterwards altered as he remembered being obliged to shorten the axles of a former engine to work on a road the same guage. He was also aware that the Tender wheels were 1" less guage than the Engine but the tread of the wheels was wider and he trusted they would have done. We will however thank you to send the two axles of the Tender, their bearings and staples, and they shall be immediately altered and returned.[228]

These two letters raise questions not easily answered. The drawing for *John Watt*'s tender (modified from that for *Mountaineer*) gives the edge-rail wheel tread as 4in. wide and the gauge over the edge-rail flanges as 4ft 7⅝in., but we do not know the gauge of the engine wheels. On *Yn Barod Etto* this was 4ft 8in., with treads only 3¼in. wide. Understanding is further muddied by the late John Owen's discussion of Dowlais railways:

> In 1838 Dowlais changed the gauge from 4' 2" [plate] to 4' 8½" [edge]. We know this definitely

by a letter written from the Dowlais locomotive engineer, J. T. [sic] Rastrick, to Neath Abbey who were building the locomotive "Dowlais", to alter the gauge from 4' 2" to 4' 8½".[229]

Owen seems to have doubly misunderstood his unnamed source. There is no other hint, nor any likelihood, of the Dowlais Tramroad being converted from plate to edge rails. Most likely Rastrick's letter simply spoke of 'changing the gauge of the Dowlais locomotive to 4' 8½"' or some such phrase. Most likely Owen, unaware of the bother over *John Watt*'s gauge, assumed that the track was also altered and himself added 'from 4' 2"'. Most likely, too, unaware that in Neath Abbey parlance 'the Dowlais locomotive' meant the one currently being built or repaired for Dowlais, he mistakenly took it to mean the locomotive called *Dowlais*.

What does stand out is that these letters of 1838 are concerned only with edge rails, and it seems probable that *John Watt* had ordinary flanged wheels, not dual-purpose ones. The only purely standard-gauge locomotives hitherto built by Neath Abbey, *Camel* and *Elephant* for the Bodmin & Wadebridge, had suffered wheel and gauge problems which Charles Jordan had had to rectify[230:] hence the reference to his shortening the axles of an engine on a road of the same gauge. If this interpretation is correct, *John Watt* could not run on plate rails at all, for edge-only wheels with normal shallow flanges would foul plate rail flanges at points (see FIG.49). That, probably, is what is meant by 'it will not fit the tramroad from the village'. If so, the locomotive's edge-only career was possibly short-lived, for in December 1839 the drawings for *Yn Barod Etto*'s dual-purpose wheels were copied, perhaps to make a set to replace *John Watt*'s edge-only wheels.

General Remarks

We have little direct information about the function of individual Dowlais locomotives, but an outline picture may be deduced. At first *Perseverance*, as a rack engine and for a time the only engine, certainly hauled iron all the way from Dowlais to Abercynon. Thereafter three different classes emerge.

Mountaineer and *Charles Jordan* were six-wheelers with larger wheels (3ft 4 or 4½in. against 3ft 1in.) and no rack drive, which would put the steep Dowlais Tramroad out of bounds to them. None the less, they had lowering chimneys for Plymouth tunnel. This proves that they did run to Abercynon, but only from Penydarren End, not from Dowlais itself. That is, they traversed only the Merthyr Tramroad proper.

Dowlais also had a lowering chimney. When Dowlais quibbled over the bill, Neath Abbey replied defensively, 'The gear for raising the chimney is an extra and we thought you would make no objection to it.'[231] This implies that Dowlais had not requested it and, consequently, did not intend *Dowlais* for the Merthyr Tramroad. It therefore seems that *Perseverance*, once *Mountaineer* had arrived in 1834, and *Dowlais* were restricted to the Dowlais Tramroad, where alone their specialist rack drive was needed. Trains, in other words, changed locomotives at Penydarren End.

Yn Barod Etto and *John Watt*, four-wheelers with (apparently) non-lowering chimneys, seem to have worked only to Morlais, in the works yard, and perhaps towards the coal mines. Only they were capable of running on edge rail. True, all the tenders of which details survive had dual-purpose wheels – *Mountaineer*'s on the Merthyr Tramroad, *Dowlais*'s on the Dowlais, and *John Watt*'s on the Morlais – but this was probably in the interests of interchangeability.

*   *   *   *

If we ignore the few and short-lived earlier examples, the two locomotives completed by Stephensons in 1829 were the first in Wales. We do not know precisely what, beyond the current railway fever, prompted Penydarren and Tredegar to acquire them, but during the next two years at least ten more were put to work in south Wales. Thus, in ordering *Perseverance* in late 1831, Josiah John Guest was jumping on a bandwagon. He was mechanically inclined, and William Crawshay II of Cyfarthfa was even more enthusiastic. Penydarren, however, lost interest, possibly because William Forman died in 1829, while Plymouth, under the conservative and anti-mechanical Anthony Hill, had no early engines at all.

Of the Dowlais engineers responsible for locomotives we know little. Most of the Neath Abbey letters are addressed to Thomas Evans the agent, who doubtless passed them on to the relevant engineer. 'The very skilful engineer Mr Gardner' mentioned by the *Hereford Times* in 1832 is otherwise unknown. Local tradition credited Adrian Stephens, the Cornish-born engineer in charge of Dowlais's mills and blowing engines from about 1827, with designing the first locomotive there.[232] Although his name does not appear in the correspondence with Neath Abbey, he could well have been responsible at least for the order. But the same tradition continues by naming this first locomotive as *Lady Charlotte* (Guest's wife), which is beyond belief: the name is not otherwise recorded, and Lady Charlotte married Guest only in 1833. Stephens was the inventor about 1832 of the steam whistle, applied at Dowlais to stationary boilers to indicate when the water was dangerously low. There is no suggestion that he applied it to Dowlais locomotives (which were noisy enough to need no other warning of their approach), but the idea was adopted on the Liverpool & Manchester from 1835. He left Dowlais for Penydarren in 1837,[233] and in 1838 the responsible engineer at Dowlais was apparently John Watt. By 1840 orders for spares were being made by one Cope Pearse. In the 1836 dispute over the bill for *Dowlais*, Neath Abbey suggested arbitration by 'your Engineer' John Urpeth Rastrick, the famous engineer who presumably acted as a consultant, and his name recurs apropos *John Watt*'s gauge in 1838.

Whoever they were, the Dowlais engineers provided rough specifications of what they wanted, which Charles Jordan of Neath Abbey translated into actual designs. Jordan was assisted by his son Charles junior. Their superiors were the Price brothers, who doubtless kept a supervisory eye on locomotive building but did not, as far as the limited records reveal, contribute to the design. Most of the letters to Dowlais are signed by Nathaniel Tregelles, a cousin of the Prices and presumably the company secretary.

Neath Abbey, like the rest of the engineering fraternity of south Wales, was not in a technological vacuum but kept abreast of railway developments elsewhere. It almost certainly had a representative at Rainhill, for within a month or so, before the details of the contesting engines were published, it offered to the Liverpool & Manchester a locomotive it was building 'on Braithwaite and Ericsson's plan, but with alterations and improvements';[234] this would seem to be *Speedwell*, the first Neath Abbey locomotive and in the event bought by Thomas Prothero for the Sirhowy, which imitated *Novelty* in its bell-crank drive if in little else.[235] Neath Abbey also borrowed from the north the metallic piston packing and the water tube, and in 1832 it adopted the multi-tubular boiler and the smokebox.

That having been said, its technical approach in the 1830s, though undoubtedly ingenious, tended towards the conservative. In their flue-type fireboxes, vertical or steeply-inclined cylinders and gear-driven valve motion, its engines conformed more to Stephenson practice of the later 1820s (still being applied by Hackworth on the Stockton & Darlington) than to the current state-of-the-art Stephenson and Bury schools which favoured separate fireboxes, horizontal cylinders and eccentrics. The point is that, in setting out to produce sturdy machines for use on awkward tramroads, Neath Abbey did not pretend to be in the forefront of locomotive design. In the duty required of them, its products were the counterparts of Hackworth's slow mineral locomotives, not of the passenger engines which pioneered the main developments. It was, in fact, that great rarity of early days, a firm which specialised in industrial locomotives when almost all its contemporaries supplied public railways.

* * * *

The exact stages by which Dowlais moved into the Railway Age are obscure. Guest was well aware of trends elsewhere. He was consulted over rails for the Stockton & Darlington and invited to tender for their supply.[236] As early as 1824 a South Wales Railway to London was suggested,[237] and in 1828 a future need for railways feeding down the valleys to Cardiff was forecast.[238] Dowlais must have seen the standard gauge on the horizon in 1832 when it specified edge/plate wheels for its second locomotive. In 1833 Josiah John Guest chaired a meeting at Merthyr to discuss plans for a railway from London,[239] and next year Brunel made his first survey for a Taff Vale Railway. In 1835 Dowlais bought its first standard-gauge locomotive. The TVR obtained its act in 1836, with Guest as its first chairman and a major shareholder, and was opened to Merthyr in 1841. Yet for a decade, despite the TVR's powers to make branches to the ironworks and despite a boom in the iron trade, Dowlais remained unconnected and continued to use the old tramroads at least as far as the TVR terminus in Merthyr. The 1840s were an anxious time, for it was very doubtful whether the landowner would renew Dowlais's lease, and capital investment consequently slowed to a trickle. But when in 1848, at the eleventh hour, the lease was renewed, a standard-gauge branch became a priority and the Dowlais Railway was opened in 1851. The Dowlais Tramroad was presumably then closed and locomotive working on the Merthyr Tramroad ceased.

Within Dowlais works, and on the lines to the coal and ore mines, conversion to edge rails was piecemeal. The Morlais quarry line was, it seems, standard gauge from the start, although a map of 1851 shows it as mixed gauge. It was probably with the arrival of the first standard-gauge locomotive, the second-hand *Etna*, in 1835 that, in order to reduce the expense of replacing many plate rails and trams in one fell swoop, wrought-iron combined plate/edge rails (later known as 'Sir John Guest rails') were introduced. The locomotives ran on the edge part and the old trams on the plate part.[240] About 1840 the Bargoed Coal Road leading to newly-developed pits in Cwmbargoed was built to standard gauge, with 36 flat trucks each carrying three 2ft 8in. plateway trams between pits and furnaces.[241] Quite possibly it was locomotive-worked. By 1848 the edge railways totalled perhaps fifteen miles and the plateways a dozen miles of 'general roads' – the main arteries – and about a hundred miles in and around the various pits.[242] Traffic on all these was heavy: in 1845 80,000 tons of ore and 140,000 tons of coal were dug to supply Dowlais's needs.[243]

After *John Watt*, because of the uncertainty over the lease and the resulting financial squeeze, Dowlais bought no more new locomotives until 1851, by which time its plateways were obsolescent. No details survive of the demise of the tramroad engines. In 1840–1 several of them were given stronger frames and *Perseverance* was considerably rebuilt. An inventory of March 1848 lists only *Yn Barod Etto* (valued at £50) and *Mountaineer* (£60) plus five or six second-hand standard-gauge engines (£780 together). These all appear under the heading 'Mine Works, Colliery &c', and presumably operated in and above the works. Below the works, though the inventory mentions the Dowlais Tramroad as in existence, it strangely does not specify or value its track or locomotives.[244] But it seems likely that at least one rack engine survived to haul empties and ore from the TVR yard until 1851 when the Dowlais Railway took over. Another inventory of 1856 includes eleven standard-gauge locomotives and no plateway ones.[245]

Of the other Merthyr ironworks, Penydarren is not, after *Eclipse*, known to have used locomotives at all. It closed in 1859. Cyfarthfa was connected to the TVR and had standard-gauge engines at least from the 1850s. Plymouth, when the conservative Anthony Hill died in 1862, immediately introduced locomotives on both its standard-gauge branch off the TVR and its narrow-gauge system. This was laid with combined plate/edge rails (FIG. 36, D) on gauges of 2ft 8in. (edge) for the new locomotives – two of which were Neath Abbey-built – and 2ft 2in. (plate) for the trams.[246]

The Dowlais engines, though undeniably a vast improvement over horses in tractive effort and economy of operation, nevertheless had serious drawbacks. As with every other locomotive running on cast-iron rails – plate rails in particular – the damage they inflicted was colossal. Plates were liable to break under the 1½-ton axle load of a horse-drawn tram. One may imagine the effect of a locomotive with a 3-ton axle load, pounding with its diagonal pistons and bouncing over the joints. Francis Trevithick had experience of similar steam-worked tramroads in 1837 when it was 'necessary to send platelayers to jump from the waggon-trains to replace broken plates'.[247]

In July 1839 Anthony Hill, the treasurer of the Merthyr Tramroad, complained to Dowlais that of the 4,200 plates required on 25 March to make good the track, only 2,260 had been supplied by the three ironworks. From 1 April to 22 June about 1,600 more plates were smashed, some 1,450 of them by the Dowlais engines. No plates at all had been supplied since early June, and Hill threatened to have locomotive working stopped.[248] He was evidently overruled, but one can sympathise. The replacement of the Merthyr Tramroad by a more modern railway was quite inevitable. Yet why, as an interim measure, were the cast-iron plates not replaced with wrought-iron ones, as happened elsewhere – as, it seems, on the Gurnos Tramroad in 1831? Certainly Dowlais was rolling them for its own use by 1835.[249] But for the Merthyr Tramroad, even before that date, the writing was on the wall in the shape of the intended TVR, and the short-term benefit of new rails would hardly merit the massive capital outlay. Punishment of the cast-iron rails by the Dowlais engines therefore continued.

But the plateway engines were full of character, and their memory lingered on – 'primitive, noisy, and unable to go faster than four or five miles an hour'.[250] Wilkins' recollections in 1888 chime with the portrait of *Perseverance* painted in the next section:

The successors [to Trevithick's locomotive] were noisy screeching things, making a great clatter. The sound of the cogs, the asthmatic puffing, the clouds of smoke, and the sulphurous smell clinging around long after the engine had passed, are all part of Old Merthyr and its primitive era.[251]

A Trip behind 'Perseverance'

In 1883 one John Howells of St Athan published an account [252] – entitled, with manifest inaccuracy, 'A day with the first locomotive' – of a journey he had made as a boy behind *Perseverance* on the Merthyr Tramroad. He was something of a railway enthusiast and his description, despite its verbosity, deserves quoting at length, for it gives a rare insight into the operation of an early tramroad and a delightful portrait of a most characterful locomotive.

The date of Howells' journey can be pinned down with some confidence. The season is clear enough. It was 'a glorious summer's day' and he was fed on bogberry pudding (bogberry being cranberry which fruits in the early autumn). These two facts together point to September or, at a stretch, October. The year was evidently before 1839. It was a time when nobody wanted to go from Merthyr to Cardiff and back in a day, and his word-picture of the valley conspicuously ignores the Taff Vale Railway which impinged closely on the tramroad. From 1841, most of the passengers who suffered in the trams would surely have deserted them for the relative comforts of the TVR, and if the date were 1839–40 when it was under construction he would surely have mentioned its impact on the rural scene. But the other clues seem self-contradictory. He is talking of a time 'less than fifty years' before he wrote, which should mean 1834 or later. But by September 1834 the Merthyr Tramroad proper was being worked, it seems, by *Mountaineer*, and *Perseverance* had been relegated to the Dowlais section. The answer to this difficulty may be either a hazy memory or that he penned his article a few years before it appeared in print.

That leaves only September 1832 and September 1833. Howells' trip also coincided with a cholera epidemic. Merthyr suffered three outbreaks. The last two are much too late – 1849, when Dowlais had deserted Abercynon, and 1854, when *Perseverance* was doubtless no more. The first outbreak (which killed 160 people) lasted from 1 September to 19 November 1832, when the engine was only a few months old. September 1832 is therefore much the most likely date. Yet Howells describes *Perseverance* as filthy and apparently elderly. The solution here is perhaps that she had already acquired a patina of Merthyr grime which gave a false impression of venerable age.

Howells seems quite well acquainted with Merthyr, but when he made his trip he cannot have been there long, for he knew nothing of *Perseverance*'s arrival which must have been the talk of the town; and he did not remain there to learn of her ultimate demise. Most likely he was a visitor, staying (at a guess) with relatives. He was certainly not a native: in the whole of Britain the 1881 census records only three men of that name born in the Merthyr area at the right sort of date, and none of them sounds in the least plausible as our author. Nor do any of those born elsewhere, with a single exception. There *was* a John Howells – and only one – in St Athan, a retired and unmarried tradesman, living with his sister who ran a grocer's shop. Aged 59, he was born (at Llanmihangel nearby) in 1821 or 1822 and was therefore ten or eleven in 1832, an age which conforms with the good deeds of the superintendent at Abercynon, who would be unlikely to hold an older boy by the hand. In all probability, then, this was our author.

His article opens with some rambling thoughts on impressionable boyhood which, like a few later passages, may safely be omitted; and some of his longer paragraphs have been divided.

* * * *

Of all my early experiences of a dominating character, none have so completely warped my mind and my judgment through life as that of the first locomotive engine I was familiarly acquainted with. I say familiarly, for unbounded admiration on my part, and a kind of attractive fascination on the other, led me to miss no opportunity of watching and indulging in wistful wonderings about her, which

54. Old and new: Quaker's Yard viaduct, apparently in 1841 when the Taff Vale Railway opened. The locomotive on the Merthyr Tramroad below appears to be an 0-4-0 but some artistic licence is possible. Wash drawing attributed to Penry Williams or George Childs, reproduced from the Elton Collection by permission of the Ironbridge Gorge Museum Trust

made us familiar friends. My reason tells me that I have seen hundreds of locomotives since then, each of which was immeasurably superior to this my first love, and that at the present day such a machine as I am writing about would be a laughing-stock in the mechanical world – nay, would not be allowed to cumber the ground unless in a museum, but would be incontinently set aside and hidden out of sight. But my reply is, reason has nothing to do with a matter of this sort, which is the property of the sentimental side of one's nature ... Thus it is with me. No doubt the splendid Great Western and Great Northern locomotives, 'The Fire King', 'Flying Dutchman', and the whole tribe of them, are worthy of everything good that can be said about them. Let them by all means enjoy praise, and flattery, and fame, and keep steadily on their rails as they fly along at the rate of a mile a minute. They were built purposely to do the wonderful feats they accomplish. It was expected of them, and they do their duty. I admire them immensely myself, but I will not

permit them to pluck from my affections one that did its duties according to its build, and in the age it existed, as satisfactorily as they now do theirs. I cannot, and will not, banish an old friend from my esteem to please them. Let them go their own way, keep themselves from exploding or running off the track, whilst I retain my affection for their less accomplished, home-bred, and elderly sister, the fancy of my youth, the old 'Perseverance'.

Not long since there was an Exhibition of the Rise and Progress of Locomotive Engines at Leeds, and many ancient specimens, laid up in ordinary, graced the scene. That ancient pioneer in the railway race – Stephenson's 'Rocket', that killed Huskisson, the statesman – was there, and many others, less distinguished, withdrawn from service before they had reached bursting point.* Eagerly I looked through the catalogue of that exhibition, hoping to find the old 'Perseverance' amongst the number, but, alas, no! she was not there. I read carefully the remarks and criticisms in the Leeds papers on the various points and technicalities of the old engines exhibited, hoping by that means to arrive at an understanding of the special qualities and peculiarities of the locomotives of the 'Perseverance' period, so as to

* Howells' memory seems at fault, for no such exhibition can be traced. Should one, for *Rocket* and Leeds, read *Locomotion* and Darlington (1875), or *Locomotion* and Newcastle (Stephenson centenary, 1881)? I am grateful to John Liffen for these thoughts.

enable me to talk scientifically about my old friend; but my labour was mainly in vain. I plunged into descriptions of the improvements and changes made on Newcomen's engines by Trevithick, Blenkinsop, Chapman, Brunton, Gordon, Gurney, and others, but found nothing that applied specially to the old 'Perseverance'. Did her owners take her to pieces, and sell her parts as old iron? Or did they allow her to run the natural course which it may be presumed would be the end of all locomotives if left to themselves – that of bursting up?

Merthyr, as a locality, was honourably connected with the locomotive engine at an early period, and no history of that 'revolutionary period' can be considered complete that does not record the encouragement to practical invention given by the Dowlais Iron Company to Richard Trevithick, when they granted, in 1805, the free use of their tramway at Pant-coed-Ivor, to work his experiments upon.* The result of those trials was in the highest degree satisfactory, though poor Trevithick did not reap personally much benefit by them. It is a most remarkable fact that the embryo engine he set running on the Dowlais tram plates, notwithstanding its extreme simplicity, possessed nearly all the essential arrangements of the fleetest modern locomotive.

I regret I cannot give the original history of the 'Perseverance'. I know nothing as to where or when she was built. I think she must have been quite a middle-aged or even elderly engine, and had been *persevering* for many years before I made her acquaintance. She was the property of the Dowlais Iron Company, whose records might, perhaps, yield some trace about her, which would be worth the trouble of seeking. She was not beautiful to the view by any means, and did not pretend to be. She was covered over with a sort of black and brown corrosive eruption, as though she were internally not in a healthy state, but decidedly feverish, arising, no doubt, from the indigestible nature of her meals of coals and dirty water, and the high temperature which her vitals had to attain before she could be aroused into vigorous existence. She was not pampered, and coddled, and cleaned, and scoured, and kept free from incrustation and dirt, like the present green and gold specimens of her family; but,

notwithstanding, she did her duty well at the time I enjoyed the privilege of admiring and wondering in her presence; that duty being the dragging of a long train of trams heavily laden with iron bars, every weekday morning, from the Dowlais Works to the Glamorganshire Basin, where the bars were stowed away in barges for transmission to Cardiff by the canal, and to return in the course of the day in the van of a similar train of empty wagons. She performed this duty with sufficient punctuality, and as much alacrity as was expected or demanded of her, it being a period when no one wanted to go to London and back in one day from Merthyr, or even to Cardiff and back. That she took several hours to perform this operation is no proof of a want of appreciation of the value of time on her part, as time was then estimated. She was in advance rather than behind the age.

The tramway she travelled over was in its construction by no means conducive to speed, bearing as it did no kind of comparison with the smooth railway that the pampered locomotives of this age skim over. Its construction having been made with but slight attention to gradients or curves, there were intervals of steep ascents and descents, such as would shock the engineers of this day. The old tramway over which the 'Perseverance' travelled had, in addition to the outer lines of iron plates, an inner or central line of deep iron 'cogs' (an invention of Trevithick's),† into which fitted a cogged wheel, which worked under the body of the engine. This arrangement was intended to increase the bite of the wheels on to the metals in ascending, while it offered resistance in descending. The heavily laden trams had no brakes to them, and the engine had no power to check their speed beyond her own weight. To obviate this deficiency, a number of short stout stumps of wood were carried on the iron bars, and inserted by the attendants in going down hill into circular holes in the wheels, which caused them to drag along instead of rolling, which stumps were removed before reaching level ground. To pilot the train to its destination was, therefore, a work requiring much care and judgment.

One quality or virtue the old 'Perseverance' possessed in a supreme degree – for it is difficult to believe that any member of her kindred, either before or after her days, could compete with her in this accomplishment. This was a capacity of making her approach known to the entire neighbourhood

---

* Not entirely accurate
† Not true.

which she was about to invade. It was done not by loud whistling, as at present, but by a prodigious noise and clatter, which awakened every echo in the town of Merthyr and the surrounding hills. The liberal use she made of this virtue left no excuse open to anyone, or anything, for not getting out of her path in good time. Nor was the noise altogether superfluous, for the tramway was a favourite playground for hundreds of youngsters. At about the time Merthyr tradesmen would be at breakfast, a rumbling hollow sound might be expected to assail their ears, which gradually increased in volume as Penydarren was being passed, growing into its loudest as the 'Perseverance' and her train swept round the corner by Morlais brook, from which point it rolled like a hurricane, loud enough to wake the dead in the cemetery above (had there been any dead then to wake). Soon after the sounds began to subside, and gradually ceased altogether as the train pulled up, as it always did, just above the Court-house at the bottom of Twynrodin, for a quarter of an hour or so, to take breath and rest. There was another object which concerned the attendants in stopping at this point, for though the 'Perseverance' did not pretend to take passengers – indeed, had no conveniences whatever for doing so – yet numbers of persons did avail themselves of a lift on their way, which they were permitted to do for a few pence of beer money, if the accommodation of merely seating themselves on the iron bars was thought sufficient. Those travellers required no Bradshaw or local guide to direct them, the noisy notice given by the approach of the engine being sufficient for all purposes.

I had many times, boy-like, wistfully gazed after this 'lengthened 'lurement long drawn out'; had envied its passengers and longed for a trip with the 'Perseverance', and I had inwardly resolved that the first holiday I could procure should see me seated on the iron bars, determined to accompany my fascinating locomotive whithersoever she might choose to take me. And as 'everything comes to him that waits,' so did a day come, a glorious summer's day, when my secret longings were gratified, and a new chapter in my experience commenced. 'Anticipation's restless mood' ran away with my sleep on the night preceding, and I rose betimes, more eager for my ride than for my breakfast. In due course the rumbling sounds reached my ears, and Twynrodin Station found me awaiting the 'Perseverance', and her clattering load. I bargained with one of the guards to take me the dual journey for the modest sum of ninepence, and felt as happy as though I was bound for the Garden of the Hesperides.

There were a good many passengers spread over the length of the train, the nearest to me being a woman with a baby in her arms, and three other little ones whose anguish and cries on parting with their 'daddy', who came to see them off, were almost heartrending. This poor woman and children were being sent to their old home near Llantrisant, to escape from the fear of the cholera then raging at Merthyr, the husband and father remaining behind to win bread for them. The scene was most demonstrative in its apparent misery, though it appeared to me at the time – such is the selfishness of boyhood – as an intrusion on my enjoyment. The children cried incessantly until the noise of the train drowned the sounds, when they left off, fairly beaten on their own strong ground. The mother made quite a confidant of me, telling me everything that was nearest to her heart, which had reference chiefly to the domestic miseries which her husband would have to undergo without her presence to manage for him.

So unwilling am I to admit anything derogatory to the 'Perseverance', that I regret being obliged to state that at times she was somewhat skittish and uncertain in her conduct. She would not always start readily when invited to, or stop when requested. She would sometimes, after starting, move along in a fitful irregular manner, causing a doubt in the mind whether the mood was sportive or mischievous. On this momentous occasion she started fairly, and even smoothly; but she reserved to herself the right to display her peculiarities and idiosyncracies at any convenient opportunity during the journey. Excepting that the vast cloud of smoke and steam which she emitted was sometimes blown into the faces of her passengers by the light breeze that prevailed, causing an unpleasant sensation to eyes and throat, her progress was satisfactory enough until the Plymouth Iron Works were reached. At this point there was a long low tunnel to pass through, running apparently right underneath the blast furnaces, and here the first and only seriously unpleasant experience of the trip was obtained. The 'Perseverance' travelling very slowly, and ejecting a vast body of smoke, steam and sparks, the tunnel was completely filled, and the eyes, ears and lungs of the passengers were charged with the unpleasant mixture. The heat was intense, with a sensation of being half-roasted and parboiled at the same time. The little children were nearly asphyxiated, and had grown purple in the face, when the open air was reached once more. After this, for two or three miles things went smoothly enough. Clamorously were the Pentrebach forges, the Duffryn furnaces, and the (then) small hamlet of Troedyrhiw passed.

Shortly after a bend in the valley shut out Merthyr, with all its smoky and noisy surroundings, as completely as though it had been fifty miles away, and the clattering train seemed like an offensive invasion of the fresh pure loveliness of nature, which the Taff Valley at this point presents to the eye. Below, on the right of the steep, sloping bank, on the side of which the tramway travelled, flowed the Taff river, a shallow, dirty stream, but doing its best to induce the bright sun to cause a little shimmering on its surface. High up on the opposite bank was the canal, along which glided the slow barges, each drawn by a single horse, driven by a lad, happy as a sky-lark, carolling blithely a Welsh song. Dotted about the landscape at intervals were small white-washed farm houses, so brightly white that they literally seemed to blink in the sun's rays. But few trees of any size were to be seen, excepting in positions very difficult to get at, for the woods had all been denuded of timber to supply charcoal to the ironworks, before the invention of the hot blast . . . [but nature, he opines, rapidly recovers lost ground.]

But to return to our subject. The 'Perseverance' after having travelled satisfactorily, though slowly, for a mile or two below Troedyrhiw, began to give evidence of failing powers; and, either from fatigue, from too heavy a load, or from not being properly and sufficiently supplied in due proportions with the generators of her motive force, displayed a decided disposition to come to a standstill. There was much excitement amongst the attendants, much stirring of the fires, which produced additional smoke, followed by a few snorts and short spurts on the part of the engine, but spite of all, she came to a full stop. An unpleasant thought crossed my mind that it was possible I might be deprived of my ride and money, but I was quickly reassured by an attendant that this conduct on the part of the 'Perseverance' was not unusual, that, in fact, it had been anticipated and provided for beforehand.

The fires were heaped up, a few buckets of water were obtained and poured in, and an iron chain or cable, some forty yards long, which had peacefully lain coiled upon one of the trams, the purpose of which I had been speculating about, was requisitioned and brought into use. The 'Perseverance' was then detached from the train, the trams were forced back as closely to each other as possible, and the heavy passengers had to descend to lighten the load. One end of the chain was then made fast to the engine, and the other to the trams. With a cry of 'Hold fast', the 'Perseverance' was then started at full speed, dragging only the light weight of the chain, which, when it got to the end of its tether, by its impetus gave the trams such a violent tug that they one and all, by a succession of jerks and jolts, joined in a chase after the 'Perseverance', and for a time it seemed as though the engine and train were actually racing each other, and that the engine was getting the best of it.

This contrivance, as it well deserved, having turned out quite successful, the usual relations between engine and train were after a while resumed; the passengers remounted, and with abundant clatter the curve at Quaker's Yard was rounded and the Glamorganshire Basin reached without any further incident. Here all the passengers departed, taking their separate ways . . . [Tired and hungry after killing several hours exploring the locality,] I at last ventured to ask a benevolent looking gentleman who was superintending the shipment of iron bars into barges if he could tell me where I might get food. Instead of answering he questioned me, then took me by the hand, led me to his home, where his dinner was just being served, and there gave me mountain mutton and bogberry pudding. This kind act he probably forgot in a week, but I have stored it as one of the things I must ever feel grateful for . . . [some musings upon hospitality follow.]

The return journey had in it nothing worth chronicling – if indeed any of the day's occurrences deserve that distinction. They have, however, seemed to me to mark in some feeble degree the enormous change that less than fifty years have wrought in the Locomotive. I have thought that the picture I have tried to draw in words of the 'Perseverance' and her ways might assist the young folks born to the privileges of to-day to attain to some notion of the blessings of their lot.

Appendix: Summary List of Locomotives

Penydarren Company

Gauge: 4ft 4in. (plate rail)

—	0-4-0G	R. Trevithick	1804	SC	$8^1/_4 \times 54$	used as stationary engine from 1804
Eclipse	0-4-0	R. Stephenson	1829	IC	7×20	converted 1832 from 3ft gauge 0-6-0

Gauge: 3ft (plate rail), probably at Penydarren

—	0-6-0	R. Stephenson	1829	OC	7×20	converted 1832 to 4ft 4in. gauge 0-4-0

William (later Robert) Crawshay, Cyfartha

Gauge 3ft 1in. (plate rail)

—	?	W. Williams	1829/30			broke rails
—	2-2-0 Gurney	J. Braithwaite	1830	IC	$6 \times 17?$	'all to pieces' 1831
—	2-2-0 Gurney	?	1830	IC	$6 \times 17?$	'all to pieces' 1831
possibly others for Gurnos			1831/2			
—	0-4-0ST	Neath Abbey	1871	OC	$8^1/_2 \times 16$	

(Note: the Williams 1829 locomotive intended for Rainhill and offered to the L&M probably never ran at Cyfarthfa)

Dowlais Iron Company

Gauge 4ft 4in. (plate rail)

Perseverance	0-6-0G rack	Neath Abbey	1832	OC	$10^1/_2 \times 20$	rebuilt 1840/1 s/s by 1856
Yn Barod Etto	0-4-0	Neath Abbey	1832	OC	$8^1/_2 \times 20$	combined wheels s/s 1848–56
Mountaineer	0-6-0	Neath Abbey	1834	OC	$8^1/_2 \times 20$	s/s 1848–56
No.4 *Dowlais*	0-6-0G rack	Neath Abbey	1836	OC	$8^1/_2 \times 18$	s/s by 1856
No.5 *Charles Jordan*	0-6-0	Neath Abbey	1838	OC	$8^1/_2 \times 20$	s/s by 1856
No.6 *John Watt*	0-4-0	Neath Abbey	1838	OC	$8^1/_2 \times 20?$	built for edge rail only? combined wheels from 1839? s/s by 1848

G – geared
SC – single cylinder
IC/OC – inside/outside cylinders
s/s – scrapped or sold: disposal uncertain

Cylinder dimensions in feet and inches

Notes and references

PART 1
THE HISTORY

1. D. Morgan Rees, *Mines, Mills and Furnaces*, 1969, p.74
2. Madeleine Elsas (ed), *Iron in the Making: Dowlais Iron Company Letters 1782–1860*, 1960, p.vii
3. John Davies, *Cardiff and the Marquesses of Bute*, 1981, p.39
4. Rees, *Mines, Mills and Furnaces*, p.70
5. Charles Hadfield, *The Canals of South Wales and the Border*, 2nd edition, 1967, p.89 gives the date as 'about 1777'. Theophilus Jones, *A History of the County of Brecknock, Volume 1*, 1909, p.140 gives it as 1780
6. Margaret S. Taylor, 'The Penydarren ironworks 1784–1859', in: Stewart Williams (ed), *Glamorgan Historian, Volume 3*, 1966, pp.75–88
7. William Rees, *Industry before the Industrial Revolution*, 1968, pp.309, 652
8. Taylor, 'Penydarren ironworks'
9. Hadfield, *Canals of South Wales*, p.90
10. Hadfield, *Canals of South Wales*, p.91
11. Cardiff Central Library: Certified copy of Minutes of the Glamorganshire Canal Company, MS 5.170, p.24. The original is in the National Library of Wales
12. Glamorganshire Canal minutes, 9 October 1790
13. Glamorganshire Canal minutes, 7 May 1791
14. Glamorganshire Canal minutes, 1 June 1791
15. Elsas, *Iron in the Making*, p.148. (This, and subsequent references to this work are transcriptions from the Dowlais iron Company letters, Glamorgan Record Office DG/A. *Ed.*)
16. Elsas, *Iron in the Making*, p.171
17. R. A. Mott, 'English waggonways of the eighteenth century', *Transactions of the Newcomen Society*, 1964–5, Vol.37, pp.1–33
18. Public Record Office (hereafter PRO): Monmouthshire Canal minutes, RAIL 500/5, 26 March 1793, 8 January 1794
19. 'Report of the Commissioners of Railways for the Year 1849', PP 1850 XXXI. p.170; Gordon Rattenbury, *Tramroads of the Brecknock & Abergavenny Canal*, 1980, p.60
20. Glamorganshire Canal minutes, 18 June 1791
21. Elsas, *Iron in the Making*, p.149
22. Glamorganshire Canal minutes, 26 January 1793
23. Glamorganshire Canal minutes, 5 June 1793
24. Elsas, *Iron in the Making*, p.151
25. Elsas, *Iron in the Making*, pp.151–2
26. National Library of Wales (hereafter NLW), Maybery 155
27. Glamorgan Record Office (hereafter GRO), DG/F1/52
28. GRO, DG/P1/222
29. Information kindly supplied by Mr J. A. Owen, one time manager of the British Steel Corporation plant at Dowlais, together with a copy of the plan
30. Full details of the early locomotives of the Dowlais Iron Co. are given by M. J. T. Lewis, 'Steam on the Penydarren', originally published as *Industrial Railway Review*, April 1975,
No.59. A revised version of this paper forms the second part of the present work
31. GRO, DG/P 39
32. NLW, Maybery 1890
33. NLW, Maybery 70
34. NLW, Maybery 109
35. GRO, Q/D/P 49
36. Lewis, 'Steam on the Penydarren', pp.15–16
37. Elsas, *Iron in the Making*, p.151–2
38. NLW, Maybery 155
39. Held in GRO
40. GRO, DG/F1/40
41. GRO, DG/F1
42. George Yates, *Map of Glamorgan*, 1799 shows 'Tora Van' at approximately SO 081073, a point shown on later maps as 'Twyn y Wain House'
43. GRO, DG/P 226
44. GRO, DG/P 187
45. George Overton, *A Description of the Faults or Dykes of the Mineral Basin of South Wales, Part 1*, 1825, p.43. Part 2 does not appear to have been written
46. Overton, *South Wales Mineral Basin*, pp.43–4
47. GRO, DG/P 128
48. J. A. Owen, *The History of the Dowlais Iron Works 1759–1970*, 1977, p.135
49. GRO, DPL/733
50. Owen, *Dowlais Iron Works*, p.155
51. Memorial in Llandetty church, Breconshire
52. GRO, Q/D/P/61
53. Held in GRO
54. D. S. M. Barrie, *The Brecon & Merthyr Railway*, 1957, p.118
55. Glamorganshire Canal minutes, 30 April 1792
56. NLW, Maybery 2460
57. NLW, Maybery 1889, fol.40
58. NLW, Maybery 2466
59. NLW, Maybery 91
60. Joseph Priestley, *Historical Account of the Navigable Rivers, Canals and Railways throughout Great Britain*, 1831, p.302
61. NLW, Maybery 2514
62. Cardiff Central Library, MS 3.788, p.34
63. NLW, Maybery 2514
64. NLW, Maybery 2524
65. NLW, Maybery 109
66. GRO, DPL/733
67. Held in GRO
68. S. R. Hughes and D. B. Hague, 'Pont y Cafnau: the first iron railway bridge and aqueduct?', *Bulletin of the Association for Industrial Archaeology*, 1982, Vol.9, No.4, pp.3–4
69. Davies, *Cardiff and the Marquesses of Bute*, p.39
70. NLW, Maybery 1221, 1912, 1913
71. PRO, RAIL 500/5, 21 December 1798
72. Quoted by Charles Wilkins, *The South Wales Coal Trade*, 1888, p.183
73. GRO, Q/D/P/8b
74. Hadfield, *Canals of South Wales*, p.94
75. Glamorganshire Canal minutes, 26 June 1799
76. NLW, Maybery 109
77. Glamorganshire Canal minutes, 1 March 1800
78. GRO/A/A-T (1800), fol 9. It is not known if this James Barnes was the man who engineered the Carmarthenshire Railway or Tramroad in 1800. It is reasonably
certain that he is the same man who made a survey of the Sirhowy Tramroad in November 1800 (PRO, RAIL 500/44/5) and contracted for the construction of inclines near Pontypool in 1802 (PRO, RAIL 500/44/14). It is doubtful if he is the same as the man who was engineer to several canals in the Midlands
79. NLW, Maybery 1890
80. NLW, Maybery 104
81. NLW, Maybery 109
82. Lewis, 'Steam on the Penydarren', p.13
83. Joan M. Eyles, 'William Smith, Richard Trevithick and Samuel Homfray: their correspondence on steam engines', *Transactions of the Newcomen Society*, 1970–1, Vol.43, p.141.
84. Glamorganshire Canal minutes, 10 October 1809
85. GRO, BC/GCA/2, p.117. I am indebted to Mr Stephen Rowson for bringing this to my notice
86. Elsas, *Iron in the Making*, p.151
87. Elsas, *Iron in the Making*, p.152
88. Stanley Mercer, 'Trevithick and the Merthyr Tramroad', *Transactions of the Newcomen Society*, 1947–9, Vol.26, plate XVII
89. Rees, *Mines, Mills and Furnaces*, p.70
90. NLW, Maybery 3760
91. NLW, Maybery 2249
92. NLW, Maybery 3286
93. NLW, Maybery 116
94. NLW, Maybery 2595
95. NLW, Maybery 2603
96. NLW, Maybery 3880
97. NLW, Maybery 2598
98. NLW, Maybery 79
99. NLW, Maybery 117
100. NLW, Maybery 118
101. Hadfield, *Canals of South Wales*, p.100
102. Glamorganshire Canal minutes, 6 June 1821
103. Glamorganshire Canal minutes, 13 February 1834; Hadfield, *Canals of South Wales*, p.101
104. Glamorganshire Canal minutes, 27 February 1823
105. NLW, Maybery 2105
106. GRO, Q/D/P/24
107. NLW, Maybery 2262
108. L. T. C. Rolt, *Isambard Kingdom Brunel*, 1957, p.81
109. GRO, Q/D/P/52
110. GRO, Q/D/P/61
111. Rolt, *Brunel*, p.84
112. Elsas, *Iron in the Making*, p.166
113. Elsas, *Iron in the Making*, p.152
114. GRO, DG/F1/52
115. *Railway Magazine*, March 1951, p.207
116. GRO, DG/C8/12
117. GRO, DG/C8/9
118. Elsas, *Iron in the Making*, p.viii
119. NLW, Maybery 2413
120. NLW, Maybery 2415
121. NLW, Maybery 2416
122. Mercer, 'Trevithick and the Merthyr Tramroad', p.101
123. GRO, DG/F1

PART 2
THE LOCOMOTIVES

124. M. J. T. Lewis, 'Steam on the Penydarren', *Industrial Railway Record* (hereafter *IRR*), 1975, No.59
125. A small selection is published in Madeleine Elsas, *Iron in the Making: Dowlais Iron Company Letters 1782–1860*, 1960
126. George Overton, *A Description of the Faults or Dykes of the Mineral Basin of South Wales, Part 1*, 1825, for example, employs the railroad/tramroad distinction throughout his book, although others were less punctilious
127. For plateway track in south Wales see John van Laun, *Early Limestone Railways*, 2001, especially pp.205–15
128. Height and width as given by the Neath Abbey locomotive drawings. W. L. Davies (*The Bridges of Merthyr Tydfil*, 1992, p.155) measured it as 8ft 5in. wide and 8ft 4in. high. About 1860 the tunnel was extended for 80 yards southwards, with a more generous bore
129. Overton, *South Wales Mineral Basin*, p.44
130. *The Cambrian*, 18 August 1832; Stanley Mercer, 'Trevithick and the Merthyr Tramroad', *Transactions of the Newcomen Society* (hereafter *TNS*), 1947–9, Vol.26, p.91
131. 1805 (output): Philip Riden and John G. Owen, *British Blast Furnace Statistics 1790–1980*, 1995. 1820–40 (carried on canal below Abercynon, Cyfarthfa figures include Hirwaun): Harry Scrivenor, *History of the Iron Trade*, repr 1967, pp.124, 257
132. Overton, *South Wales Mineral Basin*, pp.48–9
133. Richard Hayman, *Working Iron in Merthyr Tydfil*, 1989, p.32
134. Frequently reproduced, for example in Hayman, *Working Iron*, p.17 and Peter Lord, *The Visual Culture of Wales: Industrial Society*, 1998, Fig.29. For a later version of the bogie tram see Glamorgan Record Office (hereafter GRO), DG/P p.127
135. Eric T. Svedenstierna, *Svedenstierna's Tour Great Britain 1802–3*, 1973, p.55. Overton, *South Wales Mineral Basin*, p.44 gives the same load.
136. Charles Hadfield, *The Canals of South Wales and the Border*, 2nd edition, 1967, p.109
137. Davies, *Bridges*, p.156
138. van Laun, *Limestone Railways*, p.156
139. van Laun, *Limestone Railways*, p.169–70
140. van Laun, *Limestone Railways*, p.174
141. Overton, *South Wales Mineral Basin*, p.45
142. van Laun, *Limestone Railways*, p.155
143. GRO, DIC 1822(4), p.82
144. The principal discussions and collections of sources are: Francis Trevithick, *Life of Richard Trevithick*, 1872, Vol.1, 159–82, Vol.2, p.126 (to be used with caution); W. W. Mason, 'Trevithick's first rail locomotive', *TNS*, 1931–2, Vol.12, pp.85–103; H. W. Dickinson and A. Titley, *Richard Trevithick, the Engineer and the Man*,

1934, pp.61–70; C. F. Dendy Marshall, *A History of Railway Locomotives down to the end of the Year 1831*, 1953, pp.11–21. Unless stated otherwise, all the following material derives from these.
145. Joan M. Eyles, 'William Smith, Richard Trevithick and Samuel Homfray', *TNS*, 1970–1, Vol.43, p.141
146. Norman Kerr, *Railroadiana: Souvenir Catalogue of Books, Documents, Manuscripts, Pictures and Prints*, 1975, p.20
147. Kerr, *Railroadiana*, pp.13–15
148. Science Museum Library (hereafter SML), INV 1903-102 = MSL 210
149. Dendy Marshall, *Locomotives*, p.16
150. Mason, 'First rail locomotive', pp.90–1
151. The Coalbrookdale evidence is collected and discussed by Arthur Raistrick, *Dynasty of Ironfounders*, 1953, pp.160–8 and E. A. Forward, 'Links in the History of the Locomotive', *The Engineer*, 22 February 1952, pp.266–8. For the latest summary, Barrie Trinder, 'Recent research on early Shropshire railways', in M. J. T. Lewis (ed), *Early Railways 2: Papers from the Second International Early Railways Conference*, 2003, p.19
152. Frank Llewellyn-Jones, 'Steam and the Mumbles Railway', *TNS*, 1979-80, Vol.51, pp.143-56
153. For a list of all known early engines see Paul Reynolds, 'Tramroad locomotives in south Wales', *Railway & Canal Historical Society, Tramroad Group Occasional Papers* (hereafter *RCHS TGOP*), 2000, No.156; addenda and corrigenda, *RCHS TGOP*, 2001, Nos 159 and 161
154. Michael R. Bailey, 'Robert Stephenson & Co. 1823–1829', *TNS*, 1978-9, Vol.50, p.132
155. Bailey, 'Robert Stephenson & Co.', p.129; J. G. H. Warren, *A Century of Locomotive Building*, 1923, p.154. Dendy Marshall (*Locomotives*, pp.142–4) and others wrongly imply Forman's was No.16 Travelling Engine. The concept of an overall sequence of works numbers did not emerge until later
156. SML INV 1924-159 = ARCH:STEPH, Drawings 6 and (with slightly different valve drive) 6A
157. SML, ARCH:STEPH, Drawing 6B (wrongly dated to July 1828 by Warren, *Century*, p.157), National Railway Museum, York (hereafter NRM), Stephenson Collection, Description Book No.18, p.3
158. NRM, Stephenson Collection, Ledger f.175
159. NRM, Stephenson Collection, Ledger, 31 July 1829
160. van Laun, *Limestone Railways*, pp.162, 164
161. SML, ARCH:STEPH, Drawings 27, 27A; NRM, Stephenson Collection, Description Books No.1, p.27 and No.18, p.41 and Particulars Book
162. So the Description Book, but the drawings show only 60 tubes
163. So NRM, Stephenson Collection, Particulars Book; the drawings give 3ft 2³⁄₄in. or 3ft, The Cambrian 3 ft 4in.
164. Lewis, 'Steam on the Penydarren', pp.18, 25–6 speculated, on the basis of a defective list of early Stephenson products (*Railway Herald*, 1896), on possible later movements of locomotives to and from Penydarren and Dowlais. Dr Michael Bailey, however, persuades me that this list is too unreliable to base any arguments upon. I therefore withdraw the suggestion that *Eclipse* may have gone second-hand to the Earl of Dudley's Shut End Railway
165. The sources for Hirwaun are transcribed in *TNS*, 1921–2, Vol.2, pp.128–9, Dendy Marshall, *Locomotives*, pp.217–20 and *RCHS TGOP* 1983, No.23. For Gurney, see T. R. Harris, *Sir Goldsworthy Gurney 1793–1875*, 1975. The chassis of a Gurney drag of 1831 is preserved in the Glasgow Museum of Transport. Whether its cylinders (6in. by 17in.) and its very early Carmichael's gab reversing gear were copied on Gurney's railway locomotives is not known
166. Harris, *Gurney*, p.49; van Laun, *Limestone Railways*, pp.196–7
167. Warren, *Century*, p.173; R. H. G. Thomas, *The Liverpool & Manchester Railway*, 1980, p.65, 151
168. National Library of Wales (hereafter NLW), Cyfarthfa Box II 498, 24 Mar. 1830, Robert Moser (a London partner) to William II
169. NLW, Cyfarthfa Box II 520
170. NLW, Cyfarthfa Box II 523, 25 July 1830
171. Laurence Ince, *The Neath Abbey Iron Company*, 1984, pp.104–106. The Neath Abbey stationary engines which Ince ascribes to Cyfarthfa in 1833 (probably not built: NLW Cyfarthfa MS Vol.3, pp.127–8) and 1835 were actually for the Crawshays' new Treforest works at Pontypridd. R. W. Kidner, 'South Wales tramroads in letters', *RCHS TGOP*, 1993, No.83, wrongly assumes Price had the contract for maintaining Cyfarthfa engines
172. Lord, *Visual Culture*, p.63; portraits of Williams, Figs 71, 85
173. Chester H. Gibbons, 'History of testing machines for materials', *TNS*, 1934–5, Vol.15, pp.171–2
174. NLW, Cyfarthfa Box II 655, 3 September 1832, William Crawshay III to William II
175. van Laun, *Limestone Railways*, Fig.149. The distance over the jaws of the 'chairs' cast integrally with the deck is 2ft 9¹⁄₂in., the difference being accounted for by wooden keys between rails and jaws. By this time the original 3ft 7in. edge railroad from Gurnos had been relaid
176. Public Record Office (hereafter PRO), RAIL 371 / 1. Gurney was in negotiation with the L&M about supplying locomotives both earlier and later: Thomas, *Liverpool & Manchester*, pp.151, 172. Nothing came of any of the discussions
177. *TNS*, 1921–2, Vol.2, p.128
178. NLW, Cyfarthfa MS Vol.3, pp.17–18
179. NLW, Cyfarthfa MS Vol.3, p.21
180. NLW, Cyfarthfa MS Vol.3, pp.32–3. For some highly speculative thoughts about the ultimate fate of these Gurneys, see Rodney Weaver, 'Ancient Britons', *IRR*, 1983, No.96, pp.94–6 and *RCHS TGOP*, 1983–4, Nos 18a, 18c, 21, 22
181. *Monmouthshire Merlin*, 5 March 1831; Paul Reynolds, 'Some press reports of Monmouthshire tramroad locomotives in the 1830s', *RCHS TGOP*, 2001, No.168
182. Nicholas Wood, *A Practical Treatise on Rail-Roads*, 1st edition, 1825, p.48
183. van Laun, *Limestone Railways*, pp.184–5; cf pp.211–12
184. Dendy Marshall, *Locomotives*, p.220
185. Charles Wilkins, *The History of Merthyr Tydfil*, 1867, p.343
186. Charles Wilkins, *The South Wales Coal Trade*, 1888, p.187
187. West Glamorgan Record Office (hereafter WGRO) D/D NAI L/9/1
188. WGRO, D/D NAI L/25
189. The very last, apparently, were a Fletcher Jennings and a Vulcan built for Tredegar's line to Trevil in 1872 and 1873
190. For the firm, see Ince, *Neath Abbey Iron Co.*; for its locomotives, Laurence Ince, 'The locomotives of the Neath Abbey Iron Company', *IRR*, 1990, No.121, pp.120–31
191. The list of eight given by John A. Owen, *The History of the Dowlais Iron Works 1759–1970*, 1977, p.132 is thoroughly unreliable
192. I owe this point to Dr Michael Bailey
193. Reproduced by Dendy Marshall, *Locomotives*, Fig.89; it is no longer in the collection and its whereabouts is unknown
194. Weaver, 'Ancient Britons', pp.93–4 criticised it on another score, mistakenly assuming that the rack wheel was mounted on the bogie frame
195. WGRO, D/D NAI L/53/5
196. Warren, *Century*, pp.141, 143
197. *Engineering*, 15 November 1867, p.456; *Railway Magazine*, June 1941, p.247; Weaver, 'Ancient Britons', p.93
198. WGRO, D/D NAI L/20/1
199. Space forbids citation of all the drawing numbers for Neath Abbey engines. The WGRO catalogue offers a basic guide. Most fall in the D/D NAI L/12–20 series, but a number of untitled ones, attributable for various reasons to our locomotives, are in other series
200. Lewis, 'Steam on the Penydarren', p.20 quoted Francis Trevithick's statement (*Life*, Vol.1, p.165) that in 1837 he substituted 30 small tubes for 'the double or breeches fire-tube' of a Neath Abbey engine, by implication on the Merthyr Tramroad. *Perseverance* seemed the most likely candidate. But the locomotive, it now transpires, was not at Merthyr after all: *IRR*, 1976, No.65, pp.216–17 and 1977, No.74, p.147
201. Warren, *Century*, p.293
202. GRO, DIC 1834, p.985
203. WGRO, D/D NAI L/23/1, reproduced in Dendy Marshall, *Locomotives*, Fig.88. See also L/22/8–9 and David Bick, *The Gloucester & Cheltenham Tramroad*, 1987, p.65
204. Francis Whishaw, *The Railways of Great Britain and Ireland*, 1842, p.37
205. I withdraw my suggestion (Lewis, 'Steam on the Penydarren', p.22) that it was an overall wooden box (such as adorned *Royal William* on the Gloucester & Cheltenham Tramroad) to prevent horses being frightened by the machinery.
206. Whishaw, *Railways*, p.36
207. GRO, DIC 1832(3), p.54
208. GRO, DIC 1832(3), p.53
209. H. R. Palmer, *Description of a Railway on a New Principle* (2nd ed, 1824), p.29
210. GRO, DIC 1832(2), p.304; Elsas, *Iron in the Making*, p.182 (in part); Reynolds, 'Some press reports'; John van Laun, 'Crawshay Bailey's engine again', *RCHS TGOP*, 2001, No.169
211. GRO, DIC 1832(2), p.191; Elsas, *Iron in the Making*, p.182
212. GRO, DIC 1832(3), p.53
213. GRO, DIC 1832(3), pp.55, 56A
214. GRO, DIC 1832(3), p.58
215. GRO, DIC 1839, p.454
216. GRO, DIC 1834, pp.979, 981, 983
217. Minutes of sub-committee of management, 18 September 1835: PRO, RAIL 371 / 10. I owe this reference to Dr Michael Bailey
218. GRO, DIC 1835(4), p.489
219. GRO, DIC 1835(4), p.491
220. GRO, DIC 1835(4), p.508
221. GRO, DIC 1836(3), pp.388–90
222. *Engineering*, 15 November 1867, p.457
223. GRO, DIC 1838, p.413 (13 May 1837, wrongly filed)
224. GRO, DIC 1836(3), pp.386–7, 394
225. Weaver, 'Ancient Britons', p.92 gives further technical commentary
226. GRO, DIC 1838, p.401; Elsas, *Iron in the Making*, p.184
227. GRO, DIC 1838, p.406
228. GRO, DIC 1838, p.407–11 (letters 7 April to 10 May)
229. Owen, *Dowlais Iron Works*, pp.128, 156
230. Bodmin & Wadebridge superintendent's day book, courtesy the late Charles Clinker
231. GRO, DIC 1836(3), p.388
232. Charles Wilkins, *The History of the Iron, Steel, Tinplate and other Trades of Wales*, 1903, p.123
233. Charles E. Lee, 'Adrian Stephens: inventor of the steam whistle', *TNS*, 1949–51, Vol.27, pp.163–73
234. Thomas, *Liverpool & Manchester*, p.151
235. Weaver, 'Ancient Britons', p.90
236. Elsas, *Iron in the Making*, pp.171–4. The contract for cast-iron rails actually went to Neath Abbey, for wrought-iron to Bedlington not (as Owen, *Dowlais Iron Works*, pp.25, 155 says) to Dowlais
237. NLW, Cyfarthfa Box I 281(b)
238. Hadfield, *Canals of South Wales*, p.104
239. Hadfield, *Canals of South Wales*, p.108
240. Illustrated in C. F. Dendy Marshall, *A History of British Railways down to the Year 1830*, 1938, Fig.73; van Laun, *Limestone Railways*, Fig.14; Owen, *Dowlais Iron Works*, facing p.17 (all from Dowlais). For the name, Mercer, 'Trevithick and the Merthyr Tramroad', p.102
241. GRO, DG/P pp.129, 132
242. GRO, DG/E/8, inventory: mileages calculated very approximately from rail tonnages given
243. Owen, *Dowlais Iron Works*, p.35
244. GRO, DG/E/8
245. GRO, DIC 1855/6, p.564
246. Dean Forester, 'Mr Keeling buys a locomotive', *IRR*, 1963, No.3/4, p.60
247. Trevithick, *Life*, Vol.1, p.165
248. GRO, DIC 1839, 326, part in Elsas, *Iron in the Making*, p.152
249. Elsas, *Iron in the Making*, p.94
250. Wilkins, *Merthyr Tydfil*, p.343
251. Wilkins, *Coal Trade*, p.186
252. *Red Dragon*, 1883, Vol.3, pp.226–35

INDEX

Abercynon 30, 34–6, 41
Abermorlais tunnel
  19–22, 50

Bacon, Anthony 9, 26, 28
Bailey, Crawshay 39–40, 69
Baker, William 75–6
Barnes, James 33
Blakemore, Richard 37, 39
Braithwaite, John 60, 78
Brecon & Merthyr R.
  24–5, 43–4
Brown, 'Richard' 52
Brunel, I. K. 40, 78

Caldecott, Thomas 27
Cardiff 9, 32, 39, 40
Carno Mill 30–1
Charles Jordan 71, 74, 75–6
Church, William 35
Clark, G. T. 43–4
Copland, Patrick 31–2
Crawshay, Francis 58
Crawshay, George 59
Crawshay, Richard
  9, 10, 26–31, 34–5, 51
Crawshay, Robert 62
Crawshay, William (I)
  30, 39–40, 58
Crawshay, William (II)
  28, 58–61, 77
Cyfarthfa Castle tramroad
  28–9
Cyfarthfa ironworks
  – history 9, 10, 47–8
  – locomotives 58–62, 79, 85
  – quarries 26–8
  – tramroads 50

Dadford, Thomas
  11–13, 26, 29
Dance, Charles 60–1
Dowlais 70, 73, 75–7
Dowlais Iron Co.
  – canal wharves 13, 19, 34–6
  – colliery tramroads 50, 79
  – history 9, 22–3, 43, 47–9, 78
  – limestone tramroads
    23–5, 50, 69, 71, 79
  – locomotives 14, 63–79, 85
  – quarries 23–5, 50
Dowlais Railroad (1791)
  – gauge 13
  – history 11–15, 19, 22, 43,
    49–50
  – locomotives 14, 68, 73, 77
  – rack sections 15, 63, 68
Dowlais Railway (1851)
  25, 40, 42–3, 78
Dyffryn furnace 38, 44, 50

Eclipse 50, 54–7, 68–9
edge rails 12–13, 47, 76–7, 79
Etna 71, 79
Evans, Thomas 77

Forman, Richard 9, 10
Forman, William
  40, 55, 57, 77
Forman's engine
  See *Eclipse*

Gardner, Mr 68, 77
gauges 48
  See also *individual tramroads*
George, Watkin 29
Giddy, Davies 51, 55
Glamorganshire Canal
  – 'four mile clause' 10, 12,
    26–7
  – incorporated 10
  – and Merthyr Tramroad
    30–4, 39–40
  – proposed Dowlais branch
    10, 11, 16
  – tonnages 30–1, 39–40
  – water rights 30, 34
Guest, J. J.
  21, 36–40, 43, 77–8
Gurney, Goldsworthy 58–61
Gurnos quarries 26
Gurnos tramroad
  – gauge 29, 60
  – history 26–9, 50, 60–2, 79
Gwaunfarren 16, 22, 44

Hill, Anthony 37–8, 40–1,
  43–4, 77, 79
Hill, Richard (I) 9, 10, 26–8,
  30, 32–3, 38, 40, 51–2
Hill, Richard (II) 28, 33, 36
Hirwaun ironworks
  9, 31, 58–60
Homfray, Jeremiah 9, 28
Homfray, Samuel
  9–14, 19, 31, 39, 51–2, 55
Howells, John 80

iron ore imports 22, 40, 48

Jackson's Bridge 13, 19, 28
Jenkins, Jenkin 32–3
John Watt 70, 76–7
Jones, R. (of Birmingham) 69
Jones, Rees 52
Jordan, Charles
  63, 68, 71, 73, 76–8

Lewis, Thomas 9, 23
Liverpool & Manchester R.
  55, 58–60, 71, 78

Llewellyn, John 53
locomotives
  See names of *individual
  builders and locomotives*

Melingriffith 10, 37
Menelaus, William 53
Merthyr Tramroad
  – gauge 21, 28, 48
  – and Glamorganshire Canal
    30–4, 39–40
  – history 28, 30–4, 44, 79
  – locomotives
    34, 41, 51–5, 71, 75–9
  – maintenance
    16, 36–7, 41, 79
  – passengers 49, 80–4
  – proposed Cardiff extension
    39–40
  – tonnages 32–3, 36–9
Meyrick, William 40
Miers, John 33, 36
Monmouthshire Canal Co.
  13, 30–2
Morlais quarries (east)
  24, 50, 69, 71, 79
Morlais quarries (west)
  16, 19, 24, 28, 33, 44, 50
Mountaineer 71–2, 76–7, 79

Nant Mafon 32–3
Neath Abbey ironworks
  14, 62–79
Newfoundland (Merthyr
  Tydfil) 19–20

Overton, George
  21, 24, 33, 39, 48

Pentrebach forge
  33, 36–8, 50
Pentyrch ironworks 31
Penydarren Co.
  – canal wharves 13, 19
  – history 9, 19, 22, 43, 47–9
  – locomotives
    21, 51–7, 79, 85
  – quarries 16, 19, 33, 40
  – tramroad gauges
    16, 18, 21, 50, 55–7
  – tramroads (canal)
    14, 16, 19–22, 36, 50
  – tramroads (internal) 50
  – tramroads (limestone)
    16–19, 22, 28, 50
Penydarren Tramroad
  See *Merthyr Tramroad*
Perseverance 63–9, 79, 80–4
plate/edge rails 47, 79
plate/edge wheels 69, 71, 76

Plymouth ironworks
  – history 9, 16, 22, 44, 47–8
  – limestone 19, 22, 26–8, 33,
    43–4
  – locomotives 79
Plymouth tunnel 48, 52, 65,
  71, 76–7
Pontycafnau 29, 60
Powell, John 26, 28, 36–40
Price, Henry Habberley
  63, 78
Price, Joseph Tregelles
  58, 63, 78
Pwllyrhwyaid 12, 13

Quaker's Yard 13, 21, 30, 36,
  44, 81

rack system 14, 50, 63, 65, 68,
  73, 75, 79
Rastrick, J. U. 77–8
Rhymney Limestone R. 24–5
Rowlands, W. 38

Scale, John 37
Shettle, Amos 33, 36
Stephens, Adrian 77–8
Stephenson, Robert & Co.
  54–7, 65, 69, 71, 77

Taff Vale R. 25, 40–4, 78
Taitt, William 10–13, 21, 28,
  31–6
trams 48–9
Tredegar Iron Co. 55, 77
Trevithick, Richard
  – Coalbrookdale locomotive
    51, 55
  – Penydarren locomotive
    34, 46, 51–5
turnpike roads
  9–10, 13, 28, 30
Twynau Gwynion
  23–5, 50, 57

Vale of Neath R. 43–4

Watt, John 76, 78
Williams, William 58–61

Yn Barod Etto 69–71, 76–7, 79